THE
GARDEN
REFRESH

THE
GARDEN
REFRESH

How to Give Your Yard Big Impact
on a Small Budget

KIER HOLMES

TIMBER PRESS
Portland, Oregon

Photo credits appear on page 243.

Published in 2022 by Timber Press, Inc.

The Haseltine Building
133 S.W. Second Avenue, Suite 450
Portland, Oregon 97204-3527
timberpress.com

Printed in China on paper from responsible sources

Text and cover design by Cat Grishaver

ISBN 978-1-64326-081-5

Catalog records for this book are available from the
Library of Congress and the British Library.

contents

introduction

MY LOVE OF GARDENING—AND MY CREATIVITY AND RESOURCEFULNESS—
started as a child of hippie parents living in Marin County during the
funky 1970s. My craftsman father truly enjoyed bucking the system,
and my mother, a home gardener, enjoyed nurturing the ecosystem.
We lived in a house my father built almost exclusively from reclaimed,
salvaged finds. Featured in *Life* magazine, this ahead-of-its-time
house would go on to win *Sunset*'s Western Home of the Year award.
At our next house, my mother cared for a petite garden where I learned
about tending fruit trees, the power of perennials, and how to garden
organically.

Many years later, my parents built another home, incorporating a
much larger garden that once again was guided by ecological responsibility, embracing recycled materials and creative salvaged treasures.

Opposite and below:
My father designed the
upside-down potting
shed using cast-off
windows. He wanted it
to look as if it had been
picked up and dropped on
its side, like an element
from the *Wizard of Oz*.

With them, I helped grow, maintain, and edit their
inventive and resourceful garden, which won *Garden
Design*'s Golden Trowel in 1998. In this aesthetically
adventurous garden, I learned the importance of
reusing lumber and stone, dividing plants, pampering
pollinators, building healthy compost, and (literally)
turning gardening on its side.

I consciously and unconsciously absorbed my
parents' sentiment, practices, and ethos like leaves
absorbing sunlight. In my twenty-plus years of designing and maintaining landscapes, I carry these imagina-
tive ways of creating and caring for a garden, always

wondering how to create a beautiful, productive, and healthy garden, or refresh and update a tired one, without spending crazy amounts of cash or using an excess of our Earth's valuable natural resources.

The effects of climate change and our recent global pandemic, (which has not only restricted our movements but limited our physical contact with others) are creating a mandate for us to take action. We have a growing awareness of the need to change things up, turn things upside down, and pivot and morph in ways we never imagined. Now is the time to start buying less and enjoying more, spending less but having more. I'm reminded every day of the reasons why we need to connect with nature and the earth. One way to regain that crucial connection is through gardening, which gives us a sense of belonging to a special place while we experience the physicality of digging in soil, the instinctual nurturing of plants, the scientific approach to observing life, and a childlike sense of awe.

Historically, we have turned to our gardens in troubling times. Something about soil makes anxiety more manageable and helps us imagine better, happier, even prettier times. For a great example, see the victory gardens of World War II, in which Americans patriotically grew food at home, even in abandoned lots, to feed their families and support the troops. Today, the thing that drives people to garden isn't so much fear of hunger but hunger for tangible physical work that gives us hope for nature's (and our own) resilience.

As I write this, shelter-in-place orders are beginning to lift, but I continue to witness the ways our gardens have become and continue to provide necessary shelter—today's gardens are valuable and well-used living spaces, sanctuaries where we can escape from strange stresses and uncertain times. Don't get me wrong: taking care of a garden can be utterly stressful too, even exhausting, frustrating, and completely baffling. Yet, when we get it right, it is deeply satisfying. This is the nature of gardening and why we love it. Gardens are ever-changing experiments full of surprises.

Because the nature of gardening is a bit lawless and "it takes a village," it's undeniably useful for beginners and veterans alike to get help and learn tips and insider info. This book is that collection of inspiration and helpful tips. Some of the featured gardens were designed by me and some were created by other talented designers. Peppered throughout you'll find pro tips, top plant lists, creative suggestions, easy homemade recipes, and reasons why certain actions in the garden save money and make the earth a healthier place to live.

This book is a gift for my fellow creative gardeners who conscientiously attempt to work with nature, not against it. We study the environment, look out early for weeds, bugs, disease, flooding, drought, cold, heat, and soil changes, and quickly react to these situations with an inventive approach and natural solutions and ingredients that we already have at home. We also look to resources we have on hand or in place and think of ways to reuse them instead of tossing them out. Cultivating this awareness and responding to the nuances and changes and little dances that our gardens perform, saves us money, heartache, back pain, and time, so we can sit back and enjoy the fruits of our labor.

For me, smart gardening isn't about rushing or being cheap or cutting corners. Instead, it's about achieving a rewarding and personalized garden no matter the size of the space or budget. It's about making informed choices and spending money where it counts without sacrificing design or style.

I encourage you to start your wise and aware garden practice wherever you can, maybe even adopt a little buck-the-system attitude, add in some creativity, and see where the gardening journey takes you.

Let's dig in.

PART ONE

ASSESSING SPACE *and* RESOURCES

Chapter 1

THINKING *and* OBSERVING

THE FIRST THING TO DO BEFORE STARTING ANY GARDEN PROJECT is to look and think. Now, you might be saying, "Thinking? I thought this was a garden book, not a self-help book." Well, in my opinion, gardening books should always be shelved under self-help—but I understand your skepticism. Gardeners are a busy bunch. We like activity, movement, and getting dirty, and we usually have one hand ready to grab pruners and snip that wayward stem or fading bloom (even in other people's gardens).

But it's worth pausing at the start of any garden project—small or elaborate—for all kinds of reasons, be they financial, environmental, aesthetic, or logistical. When planning a make-over or redo of an existing garden, it's important in terms of both money and resources that you don't immediately run to the nursery, buy cartloads of plants, break out the shovels, and get planting. Your smartest move is to slow down and start with pencil and paper. I know it's not very "get your knees dirty," but this step will get your mind moving.

As a landscape designer, I always start client garden conversations with the same important question: What is the purpose of your garden?

The idea is to start with a sort of mission statement. What role does the space serve now and what do you want to accomplish with it? You'll want an answer to this question whether your area is large or small, on a city balcony or behind a brownstone. While clarifying your intentions and goals, you can also ask yourself why you're creating or changing the garden. By defining a purpose for the space(s), you can create center points around which to keep your design focused—this keeps you from spending money on plants, projects, or materials that you end up not needing or that would create a garden you're not entirely happy with.

Ask yourself, "What purpose do I want each area of my garden to serve?"

I WANT A GARDEN _____

- focused on beauty and aesthetics.
- that embraces a sustainable, environmental awareness.
- that prevents waste and pollution and conserves valuable resources.
- to support wildlife and pollinators.
- to give back more than it takes by producing food and flowers.
- that needs minimal maintenance.
- with something of interest year round.
- where I can entertain guests.
- where children can play.
- for my pets to safely roam and enjoy.

After outlining your goals, your next step should be to walk or drive around your neighborhood and look for inspiration. Notice what plants look healthy and happy in your area—especially if you live someplace with challenges like drought or deer. Scribble notes, snap photos, talk to neighbors, and ask for contractor and designer references.

Your ultimate goal is to establish a relationship with your garden—one that enriches you both—so in addition to how you want to use it, think about the kind of mood, temperament, and atmosphere you'd like to cultivate. Do you want to create a soothing space that calms the senses, or an energetic one bursting with color and activity? All this preplanning is important because it helps you create your garden space together with nature rather than against it, a sort of co-creation. Think of yourself as an author crafting a green, living story. Some of the most memorable and inspiring gardens are the ones that welcome you in then lead you along, just like a good book. Twists, turns, and surprises live around corners, and each area acts like a new chapter. Focal points and borrowed views reinforce the narrative. A good garden blurs the lines between the natural and the planned, between the wild and the cultivated, and artfully blends aesthetics with practicality. It exists not just for humans but also for a community of creature characters who enjoy and rely upon it. And, as no garden (thankfully) is static, it must have the potential and permission to change over time as it finds its own rhythm.

Opposite: This minimalist entryway requires little maintenance to stay looking sharp.

Above: A calming entrance welcomes guests (or even yourself after a long day) into your garden.

Right: Take advantage of a borrowed view to enhance the visual experience.

the wish list

A successful garden is all about matching preferences, needs, and budget with fixed site conditions like size, location, and existing elements worth keeping. But before you get too wrapped up in reality, I give you permission to make a wish list. This is your chance to act like a kid enthusiastically running down a list of dream birthday gifts (but with plants and patios instead of dollhouses and videogames). Put it all out there— really! Think big, like castle-in-the-sky big; get all your garden wishes down. Think about items you want or need and remember to include whatever will support the activities you want to do in the garden. Don't forget about unsexy items and areas, like a storage space for trash cans or a dog run. Don't worry about getting too far out because you'll come back to reality in the next step and cross off the can't-do items or maybe mark a few to save for later or add over time.

Left: Dream big, but realize you may need to implement some expensive items from your wish list in stages.

Opposite: Even garden corners can be packed with attractive edibles.

SAMPLE GARDEN WISH LIST

- Patio
- Wood deck
- Retaining wall
- Built-in barbecue
- Arbor/pergola
- Privacy hedge
- Fence
- Swimming pool
- Hot tub
- Outdoor shower
- Storage shed
- Potting bench
- Greenhouse
- Compost pile
- Twinkle lights
- Bocce ball court
- Fire pit
- Water feature
- Wildlife habitat
- Chill-out area
- Flower-cutting garden
- Herb or vegetable garden
- Rose garden
- Fruit orchard
- Rooftop garden
- Potted garden
- Water storage
- Trees
- Mini wildflower meadow
- Drought-tolerant/native garden
- Succulent garden
- Dry streambed
- Children's play area
- Chickens and a coop
- Swing or hammock
- No-mow lawn
- Tidy-looking service areas

Clockwise from top left:

A smart storage shed can keep the rest of your garden looking tidy.

Warm copper lighting fixtures help highlight the garden after the sun goes down.

A tiered hillside creates a space for growing cut flowers to enjoy or share.

An outdoor shower is the ultimate summer luxury, especially if your life involves sand, mud, or kids.

Bocce ball is a unique way to entertain guests and the playing "field" doesn't need to be watered.

Even a simple water feature adds calming and tranquil notes to a garden.

Clockwise from top:

A wildflower meadow provides cut flowers for you and an important habitat for a multitude of wildlife.

Don't underestimate the sincere pleasure of a hammock or swing in the garden.

A Corten steel planter gives a modern feel to this herb and vegetable garden.

A dry streambed evokes the serenity of water during dry seasons and provides drainage during wet ones.

Various comfy seats provide opportunities to chill out, take in the garden, or socialize.

Use zones

Make note of what areas you use and don't use, and the reasons why. Is a space frequented because it's conveniently located outside the living room, or is it rarely used because it's too far away, the grade is treacherous, or perhaps you don't appreciate the banter of your noisy neighbors? Once you pay attention to why certain areas are used more than others, you can focus your first efforts (and money) on enhancing only those spaces in which you'll actually wind up spending time.

befriend your site

After compiling your wish list, the next thing to do is observe and pay close attention to your garden site and all its quirks and nuances, watching all the areas as if they're your friends and you're observing their likes, dislikes, and habits. This is where we become garden scientists and investigators. Start watching, taking notes, and asking questions like *why* and *how* and *what if*. Make guesses and test your theories. If an idea fails, move on and try the next one. Sometimes we never solve a problem; sometimes we unfortunately uncover different problems. In the end we are always learning.

By understanding your garden and its nuances, you can take advantage of existing soil, materials, structures, exposure, and plants, then narrow in on a garden plan that works with what you have. This will save you time, effort, and resources, because you won't be forcing unnatural elements into your garden or fussing over unhappy, misplaced plants.

To help make the most out of your garden, start by drawing its layout on graph paper (be sure to label north and south) and use this to inform your notes. Each space will have its own benefits and challenges as related to the big gardening factors: sun, wind, frost, soil, slope, microclimates, and other local stressors.

Top: Even small spaces can hold a productive posse of plants.

Above: A pup-friendly garden allows for safe pet antics and minimizes gardener frustrations over trampled plantings.

Sun patterns through the seasons

Sun information is critical to a successful garden. The sun's path affects a plant's health and growth. It determines where you should plant things like shade trees or create plots for edibles. I have many new clients who think their garden gets a certain amount of sun, when, in fact, the area is much shadier or sunnier than they have estimated. This could explain why some of their plants seem to be "mysteriously" struggling. Sun patterns can be quite shifty and complex, changing with the seasons. Sometimes mountains hide the winter sun. Sometimes deciduous trees that made a garden shady in summer allow for a much sunnier space in winter. Unless the exposure of your space is obvious (I'm talking an open field or unchanging deep shade), you should always determine north and south in your garden then chart the sun's pattern throughout the day for as many months as you can.

PRO TIP
● Full sun = 6 or more hours of direct sunlight every day
◐ Part sun/part shade = 3 to 6 hours of direct sunlight every day
○ Shade = 3 (or fewer) hours of direct sunlight every day

Sun exposure can vary greatly throughout the day in different areas of the garden.

23

Wind patterns

Like us, plants get windburned. Gusty conditions can fray delicate leaves, cause trees to grow irregularly, and quickly sap moisture from soil and foliage. Observing prevailing wind patterns in your garden will help you make smart choices. Perhaps you'll want to install a windbreak (whether living or man-made) to shield a windy spot and protect delicate plants or better situate a fire pit, patio, or outdoor dining area. In windy areas, remember to stake and tie newly planted trees and think about installing ground-level drip irrigation, which is preferable to overhead sprinklers that blow water everywhere. If your garden is near the ocean, be sure to take into account salty spray, incessant wind, and the damaging effect of both.

Salty wind can be especially damaging at seaside locations.

TOP SEASIDE PLANTS

African daisy
(*Gazania* spp.)

Beach rose
(*Rosa rugosa*)

Blue fescue
(*Festuca glauca*)

Calendula
(*Calendula officinalis*)

Coast rosemary
(*Westringia fruticosa*)

Fleabane
(*Erigeron* spp.)

Hop bush
(*Dodonaea viscosa*)

Ice plant
(*Delosperma* spp.)

Lavender
(*Lavandula* spp.)

Lavender cotton
(*Santolina chamaecyparissus*)

Nasturtium
(*Tropaeolum majus*)

New Zealand
Christmas tree
(*Metrosideros excelsa*)

New Zealand flax
(*Phormium* spp.)

Russian olive
(*Elaeagnus angustifolia*)

Scented geranium
(*Pelargonium* spp.)

Sea lavender
(*Limonium platyphyllum*)

Stonecrop
(*Sedum* spp.)

Yarrow
(*Achillea millefolium*)

Knowing your hardiness zone will help you create a garden that looks its best in every season.

Frost patterns

Find out your average first and last frost date and notice where in your garden ice settles first and lingers longest. There are a few different sources for finding out your frost dates. Your local garden center should be a reliable source. Remember that this info is an average and doesn't take into account any nuanced microclimates your garden may have.

Frost information can also help you figure what zone you are in or vice versa. I'm not talking end zones, battle zones, or danger zones— in a gardening context, *zone* refers to USDA hardiness zones (and when referring to plants, *hardy* just means "able to survive winter"). The zone system, determined by the US Department of Agriculture, divides up geographic areas based on their annual minimum temperatures.

Many plant descriptions include the USDA hardiness zone or zones in which the plant can grow successfully. Knowing which zone you live in will help you make informed plant decisions. Two great resources for hardiness info include the National Gardening Association (garden.org/nga/zipzone) and the *Old Farmer's Almanac* (almanac.com/content/plant-hardiness-zones).

Always read a plant's label to learn its tolerance for cold.

Microclimates

Microclimates are areas in your garden that experience different conditions from the rest of your space. The differences can be subtle or obvious and caused by sheltered corners or exposed spots, places that get hit by frost first or stay warmer longer because of heat radiating off a building. Depending on the conditions, microclimates can aid or hinder plant growth.

Soil status

Getting to know your soil, whether it's well-draining, rocky, sandy, clay, acidic, or alkaline, will help you determine what kinds of amendments you need (if any) and get you thinking about matching the right plants to your soil type.

Remember that different parts of your garden may have different soil types. After a rain, inspect your yard for areas showing good drainage or poor. Take note of substantial puddling, hillside runoff, and roof-gutter activity, as these might be things you want to address in your garden redesign.

For more on soil, turn to chapter 12.

Plants like ornamental grasses can help stabilize a slope—a less expensive option than regrading or terracing.

Slope

Soil on a hillside is typically poor, rocky, and shallow. Watering plants thoroughly can be challenging when erosion and runoff come into play. Though it's possible to change the grade of a slope, moving soil and building retaining walls are pricey projects. Instead of battling a hill's contour, consider working with it. Many plants complement the lay of a hillside with naturally cascading habits and roots that hold soil in place to help prevent erosion.

TOP PLANTS FOR HILLSIDES AND EROSION CONTROL

Blue chalk sticks
(*Senecio mandraliscae*)

Blue sedge (*Carex flacca*)

California lilac
(*Ceanothus* spp.)

Creeping Oregon grape
(*Mahonia repens*)

Creeping raspberry
(*Rubus calycinoides*)

Creeping rosemary
(*Salvia rosmarinus* 'Prostratus')

Myoporum
(*Myoporum parvifolium*)

Rockrose (*Cistus* spp.)

Surroundings

It's important to assess any views you want accentuated or framed, any sights you want hidden (like the neighbor's yard or your parked car), and even any noise pollution you want quieted. Proper plant placement can solve many view and sound challenges. Remember to go inside your house and look out key windows to get a true sense of what you would like erased or highlighted. Please also be mindful of your neighbors and how your choices to block something unwanted might affect their own garden or deprive them of a view.

Above: A view of the garden enhances this kitchen window.

Opposite: Salvage or scrap steel, like the Corten steel panel at the back of this garden, can make an effective privacy screen that ages to an attractive rusty patina.

Maintenance

To help bring things into perspective, think about future maintenance costs in relation to the cost of your investment. How much time, effort, and money do you want to donate to your garden? Will a hired crew be helping or will you be doing the work yourself? Certain types of gardens will get your gloves dirtier and give your clippers more action than others. Vegetable and fruit gardens demand a surprising amount of attention and effort to be productive and healthy. Formal hedges and shrubs grown as topiary need routine haircuts. On the flip side, a garden growing mostly succulents is way less needy. When making choices, remember to think durable, sustainable, useful, and classic—preferably not trendy or too custom.

Dear deer

Do deer make unwanted appearances in your garden? This is a need-to-know factor. Waking up one morning to see remnants of a deer dinner party is discouraging and costly. Aside from building a sturdy high fence (eight or ten feet tall) around your garden, your best defense is choosing plants that deer don't like. Many less-tasty but attractive options exist. Look for plants with foliage that is hairy, grassy, fuzzy, fibrous, toxic, prickly, or fragranced.

Unfortunately, no plant is completely deer proof. Deer habits and appetites vary by location, even within neighborhoods. What these furry fiends devour in one yard they turn their noses up at in another. Plus, though you might make smart selections, deer—especially young ones—will sample most new plants, even the supposedly "deer-resistant" ones. This is because new shoots and buds are fresh, tender, and haven't yet developed their strong flavor, aroma, or toxicity. As the plant matures or the deer wise up (whichever comes first), the destructive nibbling will normally stop.

TOP GENERALLY DEER-RESISTANT PLANTS

Abelia (*Abelia* spp.)

Agave (*Agave* spp.)

Aloe (*Aloe* spp.)

Bleeding heart (*Dicentra spectabilis*)

Catmint (*Nepeta* spp.)

Coast rosemary (*Westringia fruticosa*)

Fern pine (*Podocarpus* spp.)

Fountain grass (*Pennisetum* spp.)

Foxglove (*Digitalis* spp.)

Hellebore (*Helleborus* spp.)

Lavender (*Lavandula* spp.)

Lavender cotton (*Santolina chamaecyparissus*)

Mat rush (*Lomandra* spp.)

New Zealand flax (*Phormium* spp.)

Red hot poker (*Kniphofia* spp.)

Rosemary (*Salvia rosmarinus*)

Salvia (*Salvia* spp.)

Stonecrop (*Sedum* spp.)

Sweet box (*Sarcococca* spp.)

Thyme (*Thymus* spp.)

If you're not sure whether a plant in your yard is deer proof, try leaving it out (still in its nursery pot) for a few nights to observe any nibbling and formulate a plan for how to protect it (or not). A store-bought deer repellent spray can shield vulnerable plants and tree trunks. Remember to reapply frequently, especially after a rain, and look for egg-based sprays, as these are effective deer repellents. Gardening with deer requires flexibility in plant choices, experimentation, and a little luck.

City circumstances

Rooftops often function as different hardiness zones than land on the street below due to wind and sun exposure.

If you live in the city, remember to consider the heat island effect, the phenomenon in which cities are much warmer than their less-urban surroundings. Cement, asphalt, and other building materials in cities retain heat; a lack of tree canopy means less cooling shade; and even the grid pattern of most streets helps make cities hotter. Growing zones for certain cities might be different from what the USDA suggests for their general region.

Besides heat, city gardens have special challenges. Plants, like humans, have difficulty handling air pollution, so if you live in an urban area, choose plants that can stand up to smog. A city garden might be protected by the buildings that surround it or vulnerable to whipping wind patterns. Much of the soil in cities is rocky, nutrient deficient, and potentially contaminated, plus many city gardens are small and will require you to use every inch of space wisely. A vertical garden with wall-hanging planters is one method of maximizing your planting opportunities. If you're a city dweller, you'll need to pay close attention to all the elements and will likely need to be creative with limited space.

AIR POLLUTION–TOLERANT PLANTS

Black-Eyed Susan
(*Rudbeckia fulgida* 'Goldstrum')

Bleeding heart
(*Dicentra spectabilis*)

Boxwood
(*Buxus sempervirens*)

Camellia
(*Camellia* spp.)

Flowering quince
(*Chaenomeles* spp.)

Maidenhair tree
(*Ginkgo biloba*)

homework time

The next step is to begin researching and doing your homework to see which items on your wish list are doable—both logistically and financially. This includes the sometimes disappointing and reality-heavy task of scaling down your wish list and rethinking your plan based on a budget. The practicality of things like climate, exposure, and grade should inform your choices just as much as what you can afford.

It can be hard to knock items off your list when they sound so charming, useful, and full of curb appeal, but if you're on a strict budget, focus on what you actually need (a level space for a grill) and not what you dream of (a built-in stainless steel outdoor kitchen). And while it's hard to resist our inner Veruca Salt—"I want a deck and I want it now!"—by avoiding hastiness and instead researching the heck out of material costs and different plant types and design elements, your project will pay off later.

There's no doubt that new landscaping can be costly, especially if you want high-end materials and large specimen plants. As a landscape designer who provides estimates to clients, I often find myself explaining how expensive plants are, that certain materials are pricier than others, and that labor costs and the expense of your own back (if you're doing the work yourself) can quickly add up. While doing your homework, get a sense of costs by calling or visiting building-supply companies, looking online for local chat boards, and asking any friends or neighbors about their recently completed garden projects. Landscaping costs can fluctuate depending on the size of your yard, where you live, the materials you choose, and the amenities you want, but your new garden doesn't have to completely rock (or sink) your financial boat. By approaching your project slowly, honestly, and smartly, you'll avoid costly mistakes.

Vertical gardening can save space in small urban gardens.

splurge on the right stuff

While the term *splurge* may have a negative reputation for being impulsive or irresponsible, calculated splurges have many benefits, the biggest being that some elements are worth spending money on up front because they save money in the long run. Some elements, like professional master plans, privacy hedges, or specimen trees, are an investment that produce a high return. Safety is another concern worth paying experts for, specifically properly designed and installed retaining walls and other load-bearing hardscape.

We all have individual preferences and notions of what would be considered a splurge. If you're considering spending a good amount of money on something, be sure you're happy with the answers to these questions:

- Will the item or project hurt your current financial situation?
- How long are you planning to use the item?
- Will the benefit be worth the cost?

TOP ITEMS WORTH THE SPLURGE

- Quality hardscape materials
- A master plan for large yards
- Grading
- Properly designed and installed retaining walls

- Durable and safe main walkways
- Nutrient-dense planting soil, amendments, and compost
- French Drains
- Specimen trees

- A privacy hedge
- An irrigation system with a smart controller

An attractive and functional walkway is worth splurging on.

Chapter 2

DREAMING *of a* REDESIGN

WE'VE ALL BEEN TEMPTED TO RIP OUT EVERYTHING AND START with a clean slate, but few of us have the budget. And even with unlimited resources, the smart move is to pause and assess what elements you already have that are working (like plants and hardscape) and what can be assimilated into your refreshed garden.

Repurposing existing materials, especially mature plants and high-quality structures, can help save your budget, keep usable materials out of the landfill, and enhance your design. Consider using any saved features like large trees, wooden or metal arbors and pergolas, or stone fountains as starting points around which to design your space.

Don't have existing elements worthy of repurposing? Chances are someone in your community does. Local Facebook groups and neighbors on the Nextdoor app can be great for finding free plants, supplies, and trusted recommendations for local help, plus it's an easy way to connect with a likeminded community. At local salvage yards and material warehouses, you could score a pallet of bricks or redwood boards for a fence at a fraction of the price of buying them new.

Hardscape choices are critical. They set the mood, give the garden structure, and provide a strong backbone on which to build plant relationships.

When you are finally ready to start designing, pick up your pencil again. My favorite technique for sketching out designs is the old-fashioned one of standing in the space with a clipboard and some (actually, lots of) tracing paper. I start by drawing a diagram of the area and any existing elements worth keeping. Then I place a piece of tracing paper over my initial drawing and mark out different shapes and patterns for patios, gardens beds, and pathways. I focus on the hardscape or bed shapes first and try to not think about plants unless something (and it always happens) jumps into my head, in which case I'll write the plant ideas down on a separate piece of paper. Once I have a sketch, I remove the tissue paper, place a new sheet on top, and sketch a completely different layout. This method helps the design process feel real-time and allows me to observe and sink into the space. After I have drawn many ideas, I put them all aside and let them simmer for a few days, then revisit all the possibilities and discover that one usually stands out as most worth pursuing.

PRO TIP
Reuse what you have by breaking up an old concrete patio and transforming the pieces into stepping stones or walls.

Chunks of concrete can be recycled to form a low and rustic retaining wall.

Focus pocus

Focal points are important in a garden because they draw the eye and move it through the landscape—the eye can rest on that point and pivot around the space. A borrowed view is a great choice, but if your space doesn't grant you one, make sure to include an internal view that can play the part. Consider using a sculpture, specimen tree, group of architectural plants, unique piece of furniture, or large urn as a focal point.

Above: An impressively sized Diego Harris sculpture draws the eye and captures the spirit of this garden.

Right: A fabulous fern-filled urn acts as a perfect focal point for this entryway.

getting good bones

When it comes to creating good bones for a garden, hardscape (structures like retaining walls, pathways, pavers, and patios) is key. These immensely important features provide substance and focus, delineate spaces, complement plants, and offer year-round interest. Hardscape can also anchor a garden, providing a constant among the ever-changing flowery, leafy performances. The only downside to these desirable hard surfaces is that they're some of the biggest budget eaters in a garden—both materials and installation can be expensive. But before you think only of price, remember to factor in qualities you need like durability, maintenance, weather resistance, permeability, and, yes, aesthetics. Different paving choices can help define separate outdoor rooms, but you'll want to ensure visual continuity by repeating the same materials in a couple different areas. You have a wide variety of materials to choose from and each has its pros and cons.

Flagstones come in a variety of sizes, shapes, and colors.

Natural stone

PROS Flagstone, bluestone, and granite are highly durable and available in a wide range of colors.

CONS Can be costly, the surface can be uneven, and mortared joints can fail if not dry set.

HERE'S A TIP A patio or pathway laid with precut geometric stone comes together more quickly than an organic shape because the pieces don't have to fit together like a complex puzzle.

Brick

PROS Rich, natural color, withstands fading, and is highly durable. Can be a successful design link between a house with brick elements and the garden.

CONS Susceptible to moss growth and weeds between the cracks. Needs a cleaning once a year with a high-pressure jet.

HERE'S A TIP Large brick patios can be expensive, so save this material for walkways or edging.

Composite decking

PROS Long-lasting, doesn't splinter, is insect repellent, resists mold and rotting, doesn't need resanding or resealing.

CONS Pricey and can get hot for bare feet.

HERE'S A TIP Made of recycled wood and polymer materials, its environmental impact is minimal.

Above: Brick is a classic walkway material that complements traditional gardens.

Right: Composite decking gives the look of wood with none of the maintenance.

Concrete

PROS Limitless design choices, highly durable, low maintenance, versatile, and doesn't fade (unless it is colored, then it will fade over time).

CONS Can eventually get hairline cracks.

HERE'S A TIP Concrete involves strip mining of rock, sand, and other minerals—its production is responsible for 8 percent of the carbon in the atmosphere. A more responsible product uses recycled fly ash in the concrete, which is the byproduct of burning pulverized coal in power plants. When mixed with lime and water, fly ash forms a compound comparable to Portland cement. When used in concrete mixes, fly ash actually creates a stronger material while needing less water than Portland cement.

Interlocking concrete pavers

PROS Permeable, long lasting, and available in a variety of styles and colors.

CONS Can fade over time and look a tad institutional.

HERE'S A TIP Avoid tumbled pavers, as this worn-in look costs extra.

Above: Pouring your own concrete enables you to press simple and unique shapes or patterns into it. My client chose *Fatsia japonica* leaves for her entryway.

Left: Concrete pavers are available in a wide variety of styles.

Opposite top: If you can find free or inexpensive broken or discard tiles, use your artistry and imagination to create a one-of-a-kind tile walkway.

Opposite bottom: Wood is a classic, comfortable option for decks.

Tile

PROS Unique designs and colors to choose from.

CONS Proper set up can be costly and glazed tile can be slippery when wet.

HERE'S A TIP Some styles use recycled materials, and repurposing broken tiles keeps them out of landfills.

Wood

PROS Has a warm, natural feeling. Less expensive if wood is locally sourced.

CONS Needs maintenance and must be kept algae-free or the surface becomes dangerously slimy and slippery.

HERE'S A TIP Wood is a smart choice when it's local and renewable, but not when it's an endangered wood (like ipe) or requires toxic stains and sealants. Choose sustainable wood like durable, rot- and insect-resistant black locust. Another choice is reclaimed teak, which is also durable and rot resistant in addition to being less dense, making installation easier and more affordable.

PRO TIP
Ipe trees, native to South America, are often illegally harvested and FSC certifications are often faked or acquired by corruption because the wood commands high prices. If you must have this wood, make sure you buy from reputable companies who source direct from Brazil.

Gravel

PROS Creates a satisfying crunchy sound when walked on, looks tidy, feels less formal, and can be installed quickly.

CONS Needs raking and topping off. Weeds can grow through it, especially if a weed barrier is not placed under it. Gravel can shift and move so it's not recommended where strollers or wheelchairs may travel.

HERE'S A TIP Gravel paired with precast pavers can be an excellent low-cost alternative to a pricier cut-stone patio.

Decomposed granite

PROS Provides a modern, clean look and allows water to drain into the ground as opposed to storm drains. Because it is finer grained than gravel, it is more stable underfoot.

CONS Needs to be refreshed. It can also stick to shoes and feet and then get tracked into the house where it scratches wood floors.

HERE'S A TIP Adding a stabilizer to decomposed granite can prevent it hitchhiking on shoes and feet.

Wood chips

PRO Makes an inexpensive and informal pathway. Looks especially at home in shady, meadow, or vegetable gardens.

CONS Can scatter and needs refreshing after a while. Weeds will grow up through it if a weed barrier is not placed beneath.

HERE'S A TIP A cost-saving and sustainable choice, wood chips are often available for free from local arborists.

Installing a gravel path is relatively easy and you can choose colors to complement neighboring plants.

Opposite: A woodchip path in a woodland garden is a natural fit.

bonus design elements

In addition to the necessary paths, patios, decks, etc., consider adding some of these decorative or highly functional architectural elements.

Mimic Mother Nature

Large rocks and boulders can help accent beds and give your garden a naturalistic feel. Make sure that the boulders in your landscape look as if they were placed naturally, like Mother Nature would have done. For the most organic look, first decide which part of the rock has the nicest face. Dig a large hole, big enough that one third of the rock will sit below ground level, then position the rock in the hole (a crowbar makes easier work of turning and positioning). Backfill around the rock with soil and add your plantings.

Trees make great partitions and privacy screens. Instead of planting a formal row of just one species, create a more natural-looking barrier by mixing in various sizes and varieties of trees and shrubs.

Getting vertical

Take advantage of the vertical space in your garden and instead of planting a traditional hedge, grow a living, edible fence, or install a trellising system to squeeze together function and food production. For example, espaliered fruit trees in narrow places can act as a natural barrier or screen while also providing fruit. Climbing plants like kiwi, passionflower, and grapes, even beans and squash, don't just provide tasty rewards they

Above: This small boulder anchors the patio and looks more settled with *Echeveria elegans* and *Anigozanthos* nestled on either side.

Opposite: In this narrow garden, trellises turn into living walls that neatly divide the space into different rooms.

also create shade and visually soften the edges of structures. Growing plants vertically improves a garden's output by training otherwise ground-consuming crops to climb, and trellised plants actually use water more efficiently, receive more sunlight, have better disease resistance (thanks to better air circulation), and are easier to monitor for pest issues. All this adds up to bigger harvests with less work and expense.

Rise up

If your soil is horrible clay, unforgivingly rock hard, or super sandy, don't give up; this is where the beauty, ease, and productiveness of an elevated garden comes in. Consider raised beds or planting in containers of all shapes and sizes. There is some expense upfront to get beds built or containers bought, but they offer big rewards.

A huge benefit raised beds and containers offer is control over their contents, allowing you to tailor soil to suit the plants you want to grow. You can rest assured that your soil is organic and free from chemicals because you purchased it and carefully read labels. Plus, raised beds and containers can be fertilized individually, which reduces the amount of fertilizer wasted. Containers are especially useful with plants that require heavy feeding such as citrus trees, azaleas, and gardenias.

Some other benefits of elevated gardening include: soil that can be worked earlier in spring because the sun warms raised areas faster; protection from burrowing critters (especially if a protective wire underlayment is installed before soil is added) and jumping pets; less strain on your back from leaning over to plant and harvest. All this, plus they add an attractive hardscape element that can fit most anywhere in the garden.

Wood is not only the most common material used for building raised beds but it's also one of the least expensive. Choose naturally rot-resistant woods like redwood or cedar so your beds will last. Always avoid wood preserved with toxic materials, like pressure-treated boards or creosote-soaked railroad ties. The main downside of wood is that it doesn't last forever—but it will serve for about ten years without noticeable rot.

Top: Curious dogs, like Coco, are not as likely to investigate and jump in raised beds.

Above: These painted wood raised beds make it easier for Jon to plant and harvest—and replant and harvest.

PRO TIP

Avoid putting regular garden soil into your containers just to save some cash. This soil will compact, squeezing out necessary oxygen and becoming a bog-like, smelly mess. To avoid problems, always buy soil formulated specially for containers or raised beds.

getting a sense

Smell, sound, taste, touch, and sight—incorporating all five senses in your design creates a dynamic and well-rounded garden experience. And your garden doesn't have to be elaborate or massive to achieve this. Small and simple choices add up to a space that is inviting and calming, gifting visitors with a sensory boost.

Smell

If I had to choose my favorite thing about plants, fragrance would be number one. I seriously seek out flowers I can eagerly poke my nose into and leaves I can gently crush between my fingers for perfumed inhales.

Fragrances invoke some of our strongest memories and emotions—my earliest childhood plant memory is smelling sweet gardenias warming up in the Southern California sun at my grandma's house. Despite its powerful link to our memories, fragrance is sometimes a forgotten element in planning a garden. Luckily, plants offer such a wide array of scents that it's easy to weave herbal and floral aromas into every garden space.

One idea for incorporating fragrance is to place fragrant plants in strategic spots around the garden, such as near entry paths and lounging areas. You can also add a sensory surprise by planting fresh-smelling ground covers between pavers—options like spicy thyme or sweet chamomile will emit a scent when stepped on. Think carefully about your fragrant plant choices near eating areas, as you might not want to smell perfumy jasmine while chowing down on smoky barbecue. And because fragrance is a completely personal matter, make sure you and your family members smell any scented plants at a nursery or botanical garden before investing in them.

The best time to appreciate a plant's perfume is on warm, humid days before noon, and the least fragrant experience happens on hot, dry days. There are also some plants that only release their loveliness as dusk falls (night phlox, tobacco plant, and night-blooming jasmine), so plant those near open windows, well-used paths, and evening gathering spots.

Some of my favorite plants for adding fragrance to a garden are scented geraniums, which emit a wide array of tempting aromas, including apple, rose, mint, citrus, and even coconut. There's no trickery or chemicals to worry about with these natural air fresheners—the plants are blessed with special glands at the base of their leaf hairs that secrete small beads of fragrant oil. *Pelargonium* 'Charity', 'Grey Lady Plymouth', and 'Attar of Roses' all have lovely rose scents, *Pelargonium quercifolium* has a spicy, sometimes piney scent, and *Pelargonium* 'Chocolate Peppermint' smells of, well, chocolaty peppermint.

Daphnes provide a welcome perfume in late winter and early spring, before most other plants begin showing off.

TOP PLANTS WITH FRAGRANT FOLIAGE

Bee balm
(*Monarda didyma*)

Catmint (*Nepeta* spp.)

Hyssop
(*Hyssopus officinalis*)

Incense cedar
(*Calocedrus decurrens*)

Lavender
(*Lavandula* spp.)

Lavender cotton
(*Santolina
chamaecyparissus*)

Lemon balm
(*Melissa officinalis*)

Lemon marigold
(*Tagetes tenuifolia*)

Lemon verbena
(*Aloysia citriodora*)

Mint (*Mentha* spp.)

Rosemary
(*Salvia rosmarinus*)

Sage
(*Salvia officinalis*)

Scented geranium
(*Pelargonium* spp.)

Sweet bay
(*Laurus nobilis*)

Thyme (*Thymus* spp.)

Yerba buena
(*Satureja douglasii*)

TOP PLANTS WITH FRAGRANT FLOWERS

Daphne
(*Daphne* spp.)

Datura (*Datura* spp.)

Fragrant sweetbox
(*Sarcococca ruscifolia*)

Gardenia
(*Gardenia jasminoides*)

Jasmine
(*Jasminum officinale*)

Lavender
(*Lavandula* spp.)

Lemon
(*Citrus limon*)

Lilac
(*Syringa vulgaris*)

Magnolia
(*Magnolia grandiflora*)

Night-blooming
jasmine
(*Cestrum nocturnum*)

Pink (*Dianthus* spp.)

Rose (*Rosa* spp.)

Sweet pea
(*Lathyrus odoratus*)

Trumpet flower
(*Brugmansia
suaveolens*)

The green leaves of this magenta-flowered pelargonium may seem basic but their unique citronella fragrance stands out.

Sound

Comforting, calming sounds enhance the benefits of spending time outdoors in a natural setting. Bird feeders and birdbaths encourage winged visitors whose chirps, chortles, and escapades add an entertaining natural musical element. The sound of water is soothing and has positive effects on a person's well-being and psyche,

Above: Gravel paths, in addition to being inexpensive, crunch when walked on, an auditory effect reminiscent of the beach.

Opposite: Kids love the irresistibly fuzzy foliage of lamb's ears (*Stachys byzantina*).

so consider adding a small water feature to your garden. Something as simple as a bubbler in a well-chosen, water-filled vessel can do the trick. For even more music, collaborate with the wind and add a subtle wind chime (though, if you position it near a neighbor's yard make sure the sound it creates doesn't bother them, or your neighbors may unfortunately turn into enemies whenever the wind blows). Even your choice of hardscape can add to your auditory tapestry. Think of the hollow sound of shoes on wood decking or the beachy crunch of gravel underfoot.

Touch

For a tactile experience, add texturally interesting plants that are fuzzy, shiny, or satiny to areas where people walk and could easily touch them. Spikey and thorny plants provide visual texture too, but plant them safely out of reach.

Don't forget about the effects of airflow and temperature on your skin. Some days you might want to feel a cooling breeze on your face, but at other times, a little shelter feels welcoming. Similarly, a warm, sunny spot can be heaven on cool days, while a relaxing spot in the cooling shade soothes overheated skin.

Taste

Maximize your space by challenging old-fashioned ideas of keeping edible and ornamental plants separate. Vegetables and fruits can be added to any garden space, even mingling among perennial beds. This way, you always have the opportunity to harvest a quick, delicious snack. Berries, snap peas, and any other crops that can be picked and popped directly into your mouth are ideal for lazy grazing since you don't need to go inside to prepare them.

Sight

Sight is, of course, the first sense most people think about when planning a garden. We all have our favorite colors and shapes (my favorite color is orange). Color is so important that I've broken it off into its own section (coming up next), but it isn't the only important garden visual.

Think of a garden at dusk. As the sun sets, certain plants transform, glowing and even sparkling when backlit by low, golden rays. When

Above: Apples and kale coexist happily with asters and dahlias even though the latter are mainly ornamental and the former are for consumption.

Opposite, clockwise from top:

Beautifully backlit smoketree (*Cotinus coggygria*)

Wispy Mexican feather grass (*Stipa tenuissima*) and assertive agave

Bright coral bark Japanese maple (*Acer palmatum* 'Sango-kaku')

Strikingly striped *Canna* 'Tropicanna'

White oakleaf hydrangea blossoms illuminate a garden as it slips into dusk.

creating a garden you're planning to frequent at the end of the day, place illuminating plants where they can catch these last hints of light. To maximize the effect, look for plants with leaves and flowers in shades of red, orange, yellow, or chartreuse that are fine, thin, and almost translucent. If your garden is shaded or in a spot that doesn't receive sun at sunset, white flowers are a good way to hold on to the last morsels of daylight, as they will stand out and glow against green backgrounds.

When you want a visual exclamation point, consider what are known as architectural plants. These aren't plants that belong inside or are used to make buildings, but rather plants that have their own architecture—bold, distinctively outlined, and strongly shaped. These stars of the show provide contrast to softer shapes and grab the viewer's focus, which can be useful if you want to direct attention to certain areas. Architectural plants are generally larger than the plants surrounding them, and, unfortunately, most are more expensive. But because they can bring a distinctive presence to a garden all year long, they are definitely worth the investment.

Opposite, clockwise from top:

This bold kangaroo paw contrasts confidently with *Agave attenuata*.

Papyrus with aeonium offers a striking geometry and focuses the eye.

Flowers don't have a monopoly on non-green colors.

Though there's nary a flower in sight, this lush, verdant border still captivates with foliage of contrasting textures and shapes.

The small, variegated leaves of abelia pop against the broad leaves of oakleaf hydrangea.

Dracaena palm

TOP ARCHITECTURAL PLANTS

Aeonium
(*Aeonium* 'Zwartkop')

Astelia
(*Astelia chathamica*
'Silver Spear')

Dracaena palm
(*Cordyline* spp.)

Honeybush
(*Melianthus major*)

Foxtail agave
(*Agave attenuata*)

Japanese aralia
(*Fatsia japonica*)

Oak leaf acanthus
(*Acanthus mollis*
'Oak Leaf') with cannas

Paper reed
(*Cyperus papyrus*)

Pygmy date palm
(*Phoenix roebelenii*)

Tasmanian tree fern
(*Dicksonia antarctica*)

Weeping Norway
spruce
(*Picea abies* 'Pendula')

Japanese aralia

Oak leaf acanthus with cannas

Honeybush

Astelia

Foxtail agave

Weeping Norway spruce

Tasmanian tree fern

Paper reed

Pygmy date palm

getting colorful

Color can be a gardener's most important design resource. And while some people naturally have an eye for hues, others either don't bother much or love the entire rainbow and can't decide on their favorites so they use them all. Choosing colors is really up to each person's tastes. Luckily, especially for the equal-opportunity color lovers, no true rules exist, and a combination one person finds to be clashing or too confrontational, another will find attractive. That's the beauty of creating a garden for yourself, not to suit other people's tastes.

I've heard garden designers talk about avoiding color chaos, about using complementary colors, and about picking a three-color palette and sticking to it. I do not subscribe to color snobbery. Strict color rules seem very limiting to me, and quite ho-hum.

Though the color wheel can be a useful reference for the color-confused, choosing garden colors is not as simple as it seems. Plants are multidimensional—many parts in addition to flowers contribute to the colors we see. A plant's stem, leaves, bark, petals, and seedheads all have colors of their own. When I think about color in a client's garden, I start by asking them what their favorite colors are and what colors they dislike, then I take into consideration any existing plants or elements in the garden that may have color, such as pots, hardscape, and the house. Last, I look at the furnishings inside a client's home to see what colors prevail—these are colors I know they already like, so it makes sense to potentially repeat them outside.

If you're designing a garden space that can be seen through a major window or set of doors, look at the colors in the interior space (couches, rugs, pillows) and consider choosing similar or complementary colors for your plants and accessories. This helps bring the outside in and makes your garden space an extension of your indoor living space.

Opposite, clockwise from top left:

Shades of burgundy, peach, and chartreuse create a creamy three-tone palette.

In this sustainable mix of succulents and grasses, color comes from foliage as well as blooms.

Iris 'Jane Phillips', *Digitalis purpurea* f. *albiflora*, *Persicaria bistorta* 'Superba', *Hesperis matronalis*, *Aquilegia*, and roses create a relaxed cottage garden based on shades of lavender, pink, and white.

Different colors have an almost magical way of eliciting different moods. Hot colors like yellow, orange, red, and bright pink stimulate and energize, while cool colors like blue, green, white, pale pink, and purple demand less attention and create a calmer feeling. Silver, gold, and variegated colors are useful for drawing the eye to a particular area or object, and white or silvery grays can act as a bridge between colors to harmonize a planting scheme. When in doubt, remember that the flowers don't care if humans think their colors "go" together or not—they create the colors to attract pollinators. Choose plants not based on wheels, theories, or sewing-circle chats, but on your likes, what you're drawn to, and what makes you smile.

Opposite, clockwise from top left:

This low retaining wall doubles as seating.

In this clever design, seating doubles as fire-wood storage.

A stacked-stone water feature visually cools this patio, masks unwanted noise, and doubles as a focal sculpture.

double time

These days, many of us have side hustles and can multitask like crazy, and so can your garden. Hardscape elements and plants can serve multiple purposes if designed and selected carefully. Beyond aesthetics, the obvious use for plants is as crops, but they can also provide additional materials, like cut flowers, seeds, and decorations. Many fruit trees produce flowers as well as fruit, your architectural shrubs might also flower, and edibles such as rosemary or evergreen blueberries can form low-growing perennial hedges. When you think of ways for garden elements to serve many jobs, you save money by not having to purchase or build redundant items, and you allow each element to provide maximum benefit to you and the environment.

After breadseed poppy blooms fade, their seed-pods make for beautiful and interesting decorations and additions to cut-flower arrangements.

Getting a bright idea

A common mistake when planning out a garden is to only visualize how the space will look during the day. If not well illuminated, a beautiful garden can feel unsafe or unwelcoming as day fades to darkness. Adding low-watt exterior lighting that highlights plants, architectural features, and hardscape elements is a good solution. Lighting can create drama and different moods, extend the amount of time you can enjoy your garden—especially for evening meals—improve home security, and help people move about safely.

When a garden is viewed from inside the house, it draws the eye outward, extending the space. This is as true at night as during the day. I'm talking gentle, strategically placed individual lights, not big, parking-lot floodlights, and these don't have to be expensive or entail tremendous effort. There are many options, ranging from hardwire lights to plug-in dawn-to-dusk lights to solar-powered motion-sensing lights.

Helpful places for adding lights include decks, stairways, and paths. Stake lights are perfect for these spaces, adding warmth and charm and, most importantly, illuminating walkways to increase visibility and prevent accidents.

Accent lighting (up lights, down lights, and well lights) highlights a home's architecture and living spaces and adds a bit of drama. Up lights are especially useful for highlighting vertical elements like walls, trees, and columns. One bright idea is to sink the lights in ground, so they highlight these architectural features without revealing the light source.

Above: Path lights are available in decorative, artistic, and contemporary designs to match your garden theme.

Opposite: Simple string lights, candles, and a few uplit trees add drama and warmth to this garden.

To help save on electricity and reduce light pollution, install a timer or light sensor that determines the time of day and only turns on in the evening. Choose LED exterior lights; even though they cost more, they last a long time and use very little power. Another affordable option is solar-powered lights. These can be easily stuck in the ground where the sun heats them up all day and they give off a soft, unobtrusive glow at night.

Constant nighttime illumination can confuse migrating birds and plant-growing cycles, so choose your lighting wisely. Smart lighting only directs its glow where needed to reduce the negative impact of light pollution. Look for fixtures with an IDA (International Dark-Sky Association) or Good Neighbor seal. Low voltage, easy-to-install lighting kits are available at most building supply stores.

writing yourself a reality check

When you've got your design near finished and you're almost ready to lay out garden beds, patios, or walkways, try using a garden hose or some rope to form the outline of your design. The flexibility of these materials lets you easily change contours and dimensions, so you can try an idea and then quickly try another. Leave your preferred shapes in place for a week until you make your final decision. You can also use landscape flags or stakes to mark where you think plants and trees should go. This visual process will help you decide if you've chosen the best spots and spaced everything well. It allows you to measure and assess your final plan before purchasing materials or plants to fill it, ensuring you'll only buy what you actually need.

As you decide on what your garden space might become, you might also decide that you'll DIY your project in the interest of saving money. Before you assign yourself the role of head contractor or lead horticulturist, write yourself a reality check. Are you a skilled enough carpenter to safely build a deck on a hill? Can you frame up a large concrete patio? Do you really enjoy digging holes? If not, acknowledge that you'll likely have to let specialty contractors do at least some part of the project. Of course, it will cost you more to hire out, but we are talking about safety and long-term results. Plus, mistakes could actually cost you more in the long run if you end up needing to redo a project or buy new plants.

The likelihood of needing help is like a math problem: the more square footage you want to tackle, the more help you will probably need. Plan on leaving projects like swimming pools, extensive drainage or grading, complex electrical work, elaborate irrigation systems, retaining walls over two feet high, and large decks, patios, or concrete work to the pros.

Before any construction, call a licensed land surveyor to have your property lines surveyed to avoid encroaching on your neighbor's turf.

Top: I use simple landscape flags for marking potential plant positions.

Above: Stakes and string mark out a raised bed design to better envision its placement.

This includes finding out about easements and right-of-way. Some landscaping projects require permits. Examples might be cutting down a tree, installing plumbing or gas lines, adding new electrical wiring and circuits, adding a retaining wall over four feet high, and building a fence or deck over a certain height. City, town, and county codes vary, so always check with your local city building department or HOAs and ask which permits are required. Also, be sure to check with your city's zoning department for issues around zoning restrictions and setbacks. If your garden project requires deep holes, be sure to call your municipal utility company (dial 8-1-1 if you live in the United States) before you dig. They'll provide you with the location and depth of underground pipes, electrical wires, and septic tanks.

Remember, it's okay to call in favors if your aunt is an architect or your brother works at a nursery. I believe in the it-takes-a-village philosophy, so don't be shy about asking for help. Just know that people usually love a bottle of wine or a homemade pie as a thank you.

order of events

If your garden plan is large and elaborate, and for projects you'll be working on in stages, consider bringing in a professional at the beginning to draw a complete site plan so you can decide how phases should be ordered, divided, and implemented according to construction access. Attacking a garden plan in phases is wise if you're on a budget, but get help with deciding on an order of events, so you won't disturb or remove an improved area to install a new feature later. One important factor is to think of everything that should be buried in the ground, like irrigation, electrical chaseways, and gas pipes. Nothing is more disruptive and wasteful than drilling holes or digging trenches in finished surfaces. Finally, if you're hiring someone to work on your garden, remember that going with the lowest bid isn't always the smartest choice. Always check licenses, insurance, and references.

PART TWO

QUICK *and* EASY UPGRADES

Chapter 3

LITTLE THINGS *that* FEEL BIG

SIMILAR TO ADDING A BOW TO A PRESENT OR FROSTING A CUPCAKE, when you add smart, bold, and stylish accents to the right places, a simple space can turn into a special outdoor room. Maybe you paint your front door with a courageous color that hollers Welcome, or you add comfortable cushions to an otherwise stiff outdoor couch. Color brightens a mood, and fabulous furnishings instantly signal that visitors should sit and enjoy. Sometimes simple and small additions to your garden can make a space uniquely your own.

Opposite: A color scheme of gray, black, orange, and yellow imbues a whole outdoor bar with a contemporary feel even though just a few elements are repeated throughout.

Right: Adding just one statement detail to draw attention, such as a round swing or a bright front door, makes a whole garden feel refreshed.

pop goes the container

Need a quick burst of color? Look to brightly glazed containers or glass globes. Colorful ceramics in bold forms attract attention and act as focal points thanks to the saturation of their colors and the glossiness of their surfaces. Also, placing architectural plants in pots can make a bold statement, allowing their sculptural forms to really stand out.

When collecting containers, avoid creating potted pandemonium. Potted plants are accessories and, as with jewelry, less can be more. While it's tempting to acquire free pots from your neighbors or score a bunch at yard sales, avoid mega groupings of mismatched pots in different styles and random sizes. For harmony, create a group of three pots of similar color, style, or materials. At the end of the season, nurseries often clear inventory, and you can get a good deal on quality containers and globes.

Above left: Saturated blue planters provide immediate interest, color, and continuity on this patio.

Above right: You don't need to restrict your ceramics to pots and containers; simple globes and other art objects make lovely, reflective accents in a garden too.

Opposite: A collection of various-sized pots in the same neutral color don't compete with this vibrant red seating pod.

PRO TIP

Have a gigantic pot that would be too heavy to move if filled with soil? Fill the bottom with foam packing peanuts or blocks then top off with potting soil. Your pot will be lighter and you'll keep the unrecyclable material from a landfill. Just be sure your material is regular packing foam, not the biodegradable kind, which breaks down when wet.

73

What is the number-one killer for plants living in containers? Improper drainage. Containers must have drain holes to prevent plants from becoming waterlogged, which will cause them to rot. The larger the container, the more holes it should have. If your container bottom is solid and drain holes can't be drilled into it, be very careful with watering.

When you're first planting into a container, place paper coffee filters over the drain holes to keep the potting soil from escaping while still allowing water to drain. By the time the filters break down, the plant roots will help hold the soil in place. Raise containers on small blocks or pot feet so that water can drain fully.

Some container materials suit certain plants better than others. Terra cotta and clay pots absorb water from their contents—this helps keep the pots from becoming too wet and makes them a good choice for succulents but not for plants that like more moisture. Metal containers absorb heat from the sun and can transfer this to tender plants so be careful where you place them. Wood containers easily rot and harbor fungi, so they aren't the longest-lasting option.

well-traveled treasures

Experiment with incorporating personal treasures to help your garden reflect your personality and interests or to remind you of inspirational travels and infuse a space with a worldly essence. These items can be functional, like planters and lights, or purely ornamental. Almost any humble item, when grouped with others that are similar, can become an eye-catching collection.

These vintage watering cans and assorted metal containers might not look like much individually, but together they create a graphic display.

earning complements

Look for opportunities with fabric or paint to match or complement hues from nearby flowers or hardscape elements. This mirroring can really tie a garden scene together. For guidance, pick a theme like stylized modern, beachy bohemian, or hot tropical and stay close to the corresponding shades.

Choose fade- and weather-resistant fabrics. If your outdoor cushions will have to endure pool-soaked bodies, or you won't remember to bring them inside on a rainy day, consider water-resistant options. If you have a non-waterproof fabric you like, treat it with waterproofing spray (two coats are best).

Above: Adding pillows in a complementary shade to nearby plantings is a simple design move that can have a striking effect. Here blush pink fabric complements *Rosa* 'Super Excelsa'.

Right: A casual and colorful theme relies on a simple seating platform created of two-by-fours and wicker chairs painted to reflect the leaves of the eastern redbud tree (*Cercis canadensis* 'Forest Pansy') above.

take a seat

Well-chosen, weatherproof furniture that is both functional and comfortable can be a quick way to create a welcoming place to gather. Look on local free-exchange sites for neighbors selling or giving away tables, chairs, and benches. Sometimes furniture just needs a good cleaning and a polyurethane sealant or new coat of paint made for exterior use.

Some modern pieces, such as Acapulco chairs or round swings, are eye-catching contemporary classics that are popular enough to be frequently available on freecycle or resale sites to those who watch and wait.

made in the shade

Building a permanent pergola might be on your ultimate wish list down the road, but in the meantime, add a patio umbrella that can be moved around to chase the sun and brought down in winter. A water-resistant shade sail will also provide protection from sun and rain. Neither will have you spending too much.

Opposite: A coat of lime paint makes the familiar form of an Adirondack chair feel appropriate for a "hot tropical" theme featuring plants and accessories in shades of orange and purple, such as *Codiaeum variegatum* 'Petra', *Guzmania* spp., and *Lysimachia nummularia* 'Aurea'.

Right: An inexpensive but attractive shade sail is a good stopgap until your budget can accommodate building a permanent pergola.

Chapter 4

The UPSIDE *of* UPCYCLING

AT ITS CORE, UPCYCLING IS AN ARTISTIC ACTIVITY IN WHICH interesting new items are created from old or discarded materials. It inventively reuses simple, unwanted objects and transforms them into something of better quality, design, or environmental value. A money-conscious garden doesn't have to look plain and boring, because well-chosen upcycled items can create focal points and accessorize the space.

Reusing items has many environmentally friendly benefits. For starters, it reduces the amount of material that goes into landfills. Using existing materials also reduces production of new materials, which means reducing air pollution, water pollution, and greenhouse gas emissions. Global resources are conserved and so is your budget.

The positives of upcycling really can't be overstated. If you do the repurposing yourself, you'll often learn crafty new skills and stretch yourself creatively. If you buy upcycled items from a local artist, you're supporting the creative community and encouraging innovation. No matter what, you end up with a unique object to enjoy in your garden.

The one caveat to upcycling is that you don't want to overdo it and have your garden resemble a flea market. To avoid a jumbled look, don't crowd your space. Instead, be selective and choose only those items that have a special shape or unusual appeal. Also, while inexpensive and unique are worthy attributes, they shouldn't come at the expense of health. Make sure the recycled materials you use in an edible garden don't contain any poisons or toxins that could leach into the soil and be taken up by the plants you're going to eat.

Salvaged concrete slabs, bricks, and cobblestones create a charming cottage-style path when jig-sawed together into a walk of uniform width.

SAFETY GUIDELINES FOR UPCYCLING

· Painted, pressure-treated lumber may leach toxic chemicals into soil.

· Old railroad ties that have been treated with wood preservative, creosote, or lead-based paint can leach those chemicals.

· Don't grow food in old tires as the chemicals can leach.

· Make sure the pallets you use for food or furniture have an IPPC logo stamped on them, and only use ones marked HT (heat treated) or KD (kiln dried). Avoid pallets marked MB, as this means hazardous Methyl Bromide was used to treat the wood. Also be aware that, no matter what they're made of, pallets are sometimes used to ship chemicals, which could get absorbed into the wood, so avoid using any with mystery stains on them.

· Carry a lead paint detector or swabs when shopping at salvage yards, because you don't want to bring this toxic paint into your garden.

· Make sure you find out the history of any galvanized stock tanks you plan to use. A salvaged tank could have stored pesticides, herbicides, or other possible contaminants.

· A bit of good news: You may have been warned that galvanized troughs leach harmful amounts of zinc into soil—the worry is that acids break down the zinc coating. But, in fact, because most soil is neutral, there's little to zero leaching. For safe and worry-free planting in galvanized steel, choose neutral potting soil and plants that like neutral soil.

From top:

My crafty husband turned leftover wood planks into a simple planter.

Sea glass, broken pottery shards, and shells add personality and color.

Inexpensive wire wastebaskets are an easy and smart way to protect vulnerable crops from hungry birds and rodents.

ideas for upcycling

Whether you're creating new spaces or simply refreshing old ones, remember to work repurposed creative elements into your design. Upcycled items automatically personalize a space and stamp your signature on it.

Transform basic pallets

Shipping pallets are easy to come by and are usually tossed once their purpose is complete. Why not turn this material into a variety of garden elements, from vertical gardens to compost bins?

Below: A split and painted pallet makes an inexpensive and handy garden-tool organizer.

Below right: This beachy rolling coffee table is made from a reconfigured and painted pallet.

Take stock

Troughs, also known as galvanized stock tanks, make a smart, durable and attractive alternative to wooden raised beds or traditional pots. Not only are they easy to use, as there's no building or assembly needed, they also keep burrowing animals out, come in a variety of shapes and sizes, and, because they don't rot out like wood, they're long lasting and cost-effective. You can also paint them to match or complement another element.

Remember to make sure your stock tank has good drainage. Drill multiple holes in the bottom, add two to six inches of gravel or broken pot shards, and finally set your trough on low blocks or bricks to allow water to drain thoroughly. As a bonus, the cool, damp space under the trough provides a perfect spot for beneficial garden visitors like frogs, lizards, and salamanders.

Let your walls talk

Instead of building raised beds, retaining walls, or fences from new lumber, incorporate recycled materials for a unique look that is still functional. Logs stacked and braced with vertical supports can create unique and eye-catching designs. Gabions (galvanized cages filled with rocks) have long been used as an inexpensive method for erosion control and retaining walls—they are labor intensive to make but will last forever and can be personalized depending on the kind of fill you choose.

Opposite, clockwise from top left:

Gabions filled with reclaimed terra cotta pipes, tiles, and pots become the wall of a raised bed.

Neatly stacked logs and a well-placed portal can become a unique and modern-looking accent wall.

Salvaged planks arranged in an unexpected way become an intriguing space divider.

Embrace the power of paint

Even the most ho-hum objects can be reborn under a new coat of paint. In the same way you might choose a fabric color for pillows that complement nearby plants, you can pick a paint that either blends in with your garden or stands out. Choose objects with interesting shapes and customize them according to your own color whims.

Start seeds in ice cream cones

This is a simple, creative, and biodegradable planting project I do with the kids in my gardening club at the Mill Valley Public Library. Start with cake ice cream cones, fill them with potting soil, plant your seeds, and water as normal. After the seeds have sprouted, the cone can be planted in the ground or a larger pot where it naturally decomposes.

Above left: If a neighbor has bamboo growing out of control, offer to remove some of it for them, then paint it a vibrant favorite color and use it as sculptural edging in your own yard.

Above: A factory flooring panel becomes an outdoor sculpture when given a fresh coat of paint.

Try out tin

A tin can is great for starting seeds. Remove its label and give it a good wash, punch some drainage holes in the bottom, fill with potting soil, and voilà, a perfect seed pot. Tin cans have a nice, industrial look, so if you have some that are big enough, you might want to use them as a more permanent planter.

Repurpose plastic

Plastic containers can serve as excellent temporary garden tools if you're not ready to invest in permanent ones. Yogurt containers with holes punched in the bottom are great for starting seeds, and the plastic clamshells used to package lettuce and pastries make perfect miniature greenhouses that provide a warm, safe, and humid environment for seedlings to flourish. Just poke a few holes in the bottom and fill it with soil, plant your seeds, and pop the lid closed in between watering. Seeds sown directly in the garden can benefit from recycled plastic too. Plastic bottles cut in half or with the bottom removed make easy, simple cloches to protect young seedlings.

If you don't have a drip irrigation system, or you're away on a quick vacation, plastic bottles provide multiple ways to keep thirsty plants happy. A quart milk jug makes a fine slow-watering system. Simply use a thumbtack or nail to poke a small hole near the bottom, fill the jug with water, and set it beside your plant. Water gradually trickles out and provides a slow drink. You can also partially bury soda bottles filled with water neck down in your planters so the water drains out gradually as the soil dries.

Top: Reuse tin cans as seed-starting containers; just remember to create drain holes.

Above: Upside-down soda bottles are an easy way to keep planters watered. Partially removing the bottoms makes them easy to refill.

Fashion a hotel for bugs

Also known as an insect house, these homemade structures are part art and part habitat. They can be created from natural materials like dried twigs, stones, moss, pinecones, and bamboo canes, and they provide shelter to a variety of beneficial insects. Most activity happens in winter when insects lay their larva in the rooms for winter protection and gestation.

Insect hotels can be rustic or high-design, but all should have the same goal of providing shelter to support and attract beneficial insects that will in turn support the health of your garden.

Above: A coat of paint and some kid-size furnishings turn an unused garden shed into a charming playhouse.

Above right: A salvaged architectural window frame fitted with an inexpensive mirror reflects lollipop verbena and iceberg rose back into this garden.

Shed old ideas for play

If you have children who need a place to play, consider cleaning out and repurposing an old garden shed rather than buying or building a new playhouse. Make sure you have another place to put all the sharp objects and other gardening accessories you wouldn't want them to get into.

Mirror a view

Mirrors and reflective surfaces bounce light and create the illusion of more space. Install a mirror onto the back of a vintage window frame to add brightness and a borrowed view to an outdoor room.

Lighten up

Accent lighting doesn't have to cost a fortune and can be a creative process even using basic materials. Tea lights are a great option for inexpensive mood lighting that adds romance. Glass jars make perfect votives, paper bags with cutout patterns make lovely luminaries, and tin cans with holes or slits cut in the sides form twinkly makeshift lanterns.

Marbles and frosted glass give this evergreen's planter a wintery look year round.

Mulch madly

Personalize and elevate the look of pots and containers with unique top dressings. Instead of buying mulch, remember that almost any material can be used as a soil covering. Get creative with things you have on hand or can find on freecycle sites. Bark, gravel, and stones are always an option, but also consider marbles, shells, or colored glass for a fresh look.

Make your markers

Scour your cupboards and junk drawers for supplies to create plant labels instead of buying preprinted plant markers. Making your own labels allows you to customize for different plant varieties and planting situations. Make sure to use pencil or permanent ink that can withstand the elements (ink from regular writing pens will fade or wash away in a single season).

If you've already cleaned out your junk drawer, any old piece of wood can make for a unique plant marker.

Work with the wind

If you're a person who appreciates the sound of wind chimes, consider making your own from items you have on hand or can get for free. Children love making wind chimes from mismatched cutlery, which you can buy for pennies at thrift shops. You might also plan a day at the beach to collect items like shells and sea glass. For a wind chime that's less high-pitched than most, forage for different sizes of driftwood.

Don't contain yourself

Countless unwanted household items can be transformed into fun and functional containers for succulents, edibles, and perennials. The most popular are wine crates and barrels, metal washing tubs, bird cages, pallets, and old wheelbarrows, but almost any bucket-shaped household item can become a vessel for plants—just remember to add drain holes before planting.

Commemorate a memorable beach day with found objects whose soft sounds will always remind you of the sea and sunshine.

Clockwise from top:

Metal tubs acquire a lovely patina when used as planters, which can complement foliage.

Garage-sale colanders come with convenient ready-made drainage.

Unexpected household items create whimsical planters.

Chapter 5

MASTER *of the* MULCH

MULCHING CAN BE AN EASY PROJECT THAT MAKES GARDEN BEDS
look instantly refreshed. It can also completely change the style of beds
by swapping out bare dirt or bark chips for smooth Mexican pebbles or
gravel. Bare soil is basically a weed reserve, which translates into extra
work for the time-conscious gardener. And though mulch does help
block light from the soil so weeds can't rear their pesky heads, there are a
surprising multitude of other ways it is helpful. The idea of mulch comes
directly from forest ecosystems, in which carpets of plant material die,
decompose, and naturally nourish the soil while feeding families of tiny
beneficial organisms. It's a key player in conscientious, low-maintenance
gardening. The idea is to cover any bare ground with a layer of a permeable material so that the soil retains critical nutrients and moisture.
When applied correctly, mulch checks off a lot of thrifty-gardener boxes.

The best time to mulch is in spring after the soil warms up, because
it helps hold in the toastiness. This means, come springtime, you should
check on your garden's mulched areas and add more if the layers are
sparse and need a touch-up. Then check again on your mulch status in
late fall after all summer antics cease. A generous blanket of mulch is
ideal but don't overdo it—you want your mulch to be around two to four
inches thick. Too thin and it isn't very helpful, too thick and oxygen can't
reach the soil, causing plants to suffocate. Never pile up mulch like a
volcano against a plant's trunk as this can encourage rot, pests, and
diseases. Ideally, keep mulch six inches away from tree trunks and
shrub stems.

Mulch can unify a
garden and save time
and resources, too.

A MULTITUDE OF MULCH BENEFITS

- Reduces weeds, which saves time on maintenance and creates an environment where plants don't have to battle with weeds for water, light, and nutrients
- Reduces water evaporation, which cuts down on your need to water so often
- Keeps soil temperature cool, moist, and consistent, despite weather
- Creates plants with stronger roots
- Encourages earthworm activity
- Adds organic matter that feeds beneficial soil organisms and improves soil structure
- Controls and prevents soil erosion and runoff, especially on slopes
- Prevents soil hardening and compaction
- Prevents dust and mud bowls that kids and dogs seek out and then track into your house
- Tidies up a landscape by covering bare soil while you wait for plants to fill in, or while you wait to buy more plants as your budget allows
- Helps create a uniform look by being a visual constant throughout the garden
- Reduces splashing of soil and water onto vulnerable leaves that might become infected with soil pathogens

PRO TIP

If you're adding mulch to your garden for the first time and need a huge amount, consider getting it delivered from a landscaping supply store instead of buying it in bags. Buying in bulk is less expensive than buying stacks of individual bags from your local garden center, plus you won't have to haul and unload the heavy stuff yourself.

Wood-chip mulch keeps down weeds, conserves water, and looks tidy.

If there are any downsides to mulch it's only that most materials need to be replenished or replaced, and some can scatter about. Also, large expanses of mulch shouldn't be the endgame for your garden. Plan to use it in the interim until plants, and especially ground covers, fill in the spaces.

The question of "the best mulch" is something I get asked all the time. I wish I had a simple answer, but the choice of "best" hinges on your preferred aesthetic, your garden site (whether the land is flat or sloped), if you want organic or inorganic, and whether you live in a fire zone.

We can all agree that mulch is important, that many choices are available, and that the process of mulching seems fairly easy, but, like most things, there are nuggets of extra info and helpful hints that make the process simpler, less expensive, and more successful.

Leaves are an often-overlooked free mulch material.

organic mulches

LEAVES The ultimate, gloriously free mulch. To enhance usefulness, simply run a mower over healthy, disease-free leaves a few times to dice them up, then spread them around your garden. Chopped leaves break down quickly, feed your plants, and help the soil retain moisture. Some gardeners suggest never raking leaves, instead leaving them where they fall to decompose where Mother Nature (and the tree) intended them. This is an aesthetic choice. Maybe you don't like the messy fallen-leaf look (don't worry, most of my clients don't like it either). I practice a bit of both in my garden. If autumn's leafy cascade smothers my delicate plants, then I gently clear the leaves away, but if they aren't bothering anyone, I leave them be.

LEAF MOLD The next step beyond chopped up fresh leaves is leaf mold, which is what fallen leaves eventually turn into naturally. You can make your own from the leaves in your yard or buy it ready made. It decomposes quickly and is high in beneficial bacteria.

PINE NEEDLES A natural, free mulch that resists decomposing, which makes it long lasting. Keep in mind that pine needles are acidifying, so only use them around acid-loving plants like azaleas, blueberries, and rhododendrons. Also, the needles look more at home in a woodland garden than a modern one. Word of caution: pine needles are extremely flammable so don't spread them around your home or wood structures.

BARK NUGGETS Sometimes called micro bark, this mulch looks tidy and works okay but doesn't stay in place well—it's easily washed away in heavy rain, the nuggets taking off like little wooden boats, and it gets kicked around by active pets and kid antics. It's definitely not a good option for slopes, as it will absolutely slide downhill.

COCOA HULLS Trendy for a while, this mulch has a distinct chocolaty smell but is relatively expensive and—more importantly—is toxic to dogs.

SHREDDED BARK An inexpensive mulch that's easy to apply and effective on slopes, bark mulch doesn't add as many nutrients to soil as some other mulch choices. It can come from a variety of tree sources and provides an earthy look.

WOOD CHIPS Can be sourced for free in large quantities from local arborists or electrical companies that take down trees threatening power lines. However, if the wood supply source can't be identified, then you may be getting poison oak or poison sumac in the mix. Be sure to avoid using the black plagues of mulch: camphor and black walnut. These trees contain a chemical that discourages plant growth and even kills many plants.

Opposite top: Compost is your most nutrient-rich mulch option.

Opposite bottom: Straw is a traditional year-round mulch for strawberry beds, as it is light, loose, and keeps dirt off the fruit.

COMPOST When used as a mulch, compost adds a multitude of nutrients and improves soil structure. Earthworms will do the hard work of dragging the compost underground and mixing it into your soil—all without asking for a paycheck. Of course that means this mulch option needs to be refreshed often because it breaks down quickly. Some municipalities give compost away for free, but make sure it is not waste-derived before using it. To be on the safe side, avoid using questionable compost on edibles if you can't be entirely certain of its source.

STRAW Typically, straw is used in strawberry beds and vegetable gardens. It's slower to break down than leaves and it offers good winter protection. Double check to make sure you're purchasing straw—not hay—and that your straw is free of weed seeds, otherwise this mulch can create more weeds than it prevents. Avoid especially weedy oat straw.

SHREDDED REDWOOD Like a true native Californian, I adore redwood trees—but I detest shredded redwood, sold sometimes as gorilla-hair mulch. Sure, redwoods have their natural insect-repelling and rot-resistant qualities, and, in theory, shredded redwood mulch sounds like a good choice because it resists ant and termite infestations and lasts longer than other wood mulches, but the downsides trump the positives. Be aware that shredded redwood creates a matted, fibrous carpet that can become too dense for water to pass through, it traps moisture beneath it and contributes to fungal diseases, and, (perhaps its biggest downside), it's very flammable. If you must use it, avoid placing it within five feet of your home—especially if your home is in a wildfire area—and don't use it in an area potentially exposed to open flames.

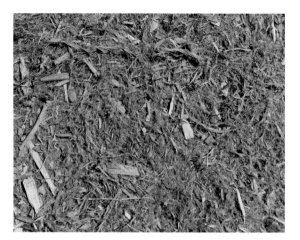

Above: There's no way to know where this mystery shredded mulch came from. Best to avoid.

Opposite top: Small stones are a good mulch match for succulents since they recall desert environments and keep foliage dry.

Opposite bottom: Slate chips are a less-popular but excellent inorganic mulch.

Some commercial chipped or shredded mulches are colored to resemble redwood and some are died black. This is actually scrap wood left over from used lumber or pallets. Avoid this mystery mulch because it could contain solvents or other chemicals that can leach out and harm plants and soil.

NEWSPAPER OR CARDBOARD A free mulch for the money- and resource-conscious gardener. Simply lay sheets of newspaper or flattened cardboard boxes down, then lay leaves or compost over the material so it won't fly away. Paper-based mulch acts like landscape fabric to suppress weeds, and it decomposes naturally and will improve your soil with time.

Cardboard lasts longer, covers larger areas, and is easier to lay down than newspaper. If you are using newspaper, use only the black and white sections. The colored inks aren't good for the garden, plus plants can't appreciate the cartoons or use the coupons.

inorganic mulches

Semipermanent mulch choices can be easy to install, and because they don't break down over time, they don't need to be reapplied every year, only refreshed a little. Stones are often used in succulent gardens because they not only look at home paired with desert growers but they also keep succulents on the drier side and provide excellent drainage. Hard mulches also offer superior fireproofing and are a smart choice when mulch is needed within five feet of a combustible structure. In fire-prone areas, routinely removing any fallen or windblown leaf litter that collects on inorganic mulch helps prevent possible small fires from igniting structures. The downside to inorganic mulches is that they are difficult to plant in once the material is spread and they don't improve soil over time.

SLATE CHIPS This relatively underused material is extremely versatile and excellent for mulching borders, containers, paths, and even pond features. Some benefits include: it's easy to install, it's durable and not altered by harsh weather (it actually looks lovely wet or dry), and it's a recycled material, which makes it more environmentally friendly than other quarried stones.

DECOMPOSED GRANITE Like gravel, but a much smaller grain and generally more stable, DG (as it's also called) is formed from the natural weathering and erosion of solid granite. It can be spread around trees and garden beds much like wood mulch, lasts longer than most other mulch materials, and won't attract pests.

ROCKS This mulch includes gravel and river stones. With a dizzying array of sizes and colors to choose from, rocks are a flexible design option. They are a smart choice for xeriscape gardens, where water is restricted, or in gardens growing succulents or other plants that need free-draining mulch to keep their stems and leaves dry. Lavender, for example, appreciates a mulching of lighter-colored gravel or stones as opposed to wood mulches that retain excess moisture.

Keep in mind that, for better or worse depending on what's planted within, rocks hold on to and radiate heat and cold. In a full-sun succulent garden mulched with stones, the extra heat from darker stones can burn sensitive succulents. Choose your stone colors carefully.

My personal pet peeve when it comes to stone mulches is that it can be a pain to clear their nooks and crannies of fallen leaves. Luckily, an electric leaf blower can help.

Top: Stones neatly fill in border edges and complement clean concrete elements.

Above: A combination of different stones creates a striking design.

living mulch

If you aren't sold on any of the organic or inorganic mulches—whether your concerns are aesthetic, financial, or both—you can choose to use low-growing plants instead. This is known as living mulch. Perennial ground covers, with their ability to spread effectively, perform many of mulch's functions, such as discouraging weeds, protecting soil, retaining moisture, and giving garden beds a particular look.

Creeping *Geranium* *×cantabrigiense* 'Biokovo' forms a living mulch under oakleaf hydrangea in this border.

the LAWN *and* SHORT OF IT

I'LL BE THE FIRST TO ADMIT THAT I LOVE THE SMELL OF A FRESHLY cut lawn. What I don't like is the nasty odor and noise pollution of gas mowers and blowers, or the idea of wasting water and chemical fertilizers, especially as they pool up on sidewalks and wash down drains. Plus, lawns create impoverished soil and an inhospitable monoculture that doesn't support wildlife or pollinators. It turns out a green lawn is actually anti-green, because when it comes to water use, the top inappropriate plant choice is the greedy lawn.

Still, I know if I took a drive through most suburbs, I would not find lawns to be an endangered species but rather alive and well fertilized. Traditional lawns are an ingrained part of American life, and it's unreasonable to think they will all just disappear, but it would be really helpful (for wildlife and your wallet) if they weren't the main feature of most yards.

Think of all the resources (water, fertilizer, gas or electricity for the mower, your precious time) that go into maintaining a lawn. Unless you've got young kids or pets actively playing on it, you should consider something less resource hungry for your new garden. At the very least, think of ways to reduce the size of your current lawn, perhaps making it a side element that complements a perennial and shrub bed. If you must have some lawn, follow the tips here to use the fewest possible resources to maintain it.

· Reduce your lawn size.
· Leave your grass clippings on the lawn, where they will decompose and create a fine mulch layer that saves moisture and is a natural nitrogen-rich fertilizer.

This home successfully uses limestone hardscape and no-mow grasses to create a welcoming but low-maintenance, low-resource-consuming yard.

- Mow when your grass is dry to keep clippings from clumping together, which slows the breakdown.
- Mow in the morning or evening so the lawn is less stressed.
- Keep your mower blades sharp so that the grass blades don't tear and turn brown at the tips.
- Set your mower blades high and let your lawn grow taller instead of opting for a harsh buzz cut. Avoid removing more than one third of your grass height because a short lawn requires more water to stay hydrated.
- Water your lawn in the morning to protect it from heat stress. Morning wind is usually calmer and the air's humidity is higher, so roots absorb water better and your grass is well hydrated by the time the heat of the day arrives.
- Irrigate your lawn with efficient multi-stream, multi-directory rotors that have a uniform spray. If you still have the old impact heads in your system, it's time to upgrade.
- Aerate and dethatch your lawn to allow water to better penetrate the soil.
- If you use an overhead sprinkler system, place an empty container (a squat tuna can works) in the center of the spray pattern; let the system run for an hour, then measure the water depth in the container. Traditional lawns need roughly one inch of water a week, unless drought restrictions are in place, in which case it might need to be less.
- Avoid synthetic fertilizers and instead apply a slow-release organic fertilizer in spring.

Above: Be bold and devote your front yard to vegetable gardens rather than lawn.

Below: No-mow fescue grasses add green, are drought tolerant, and don't require as much maintenance as traditional lawns.

turf it out

Luckily many design ideas exist to help end our collective romance with turf while still creating an attractive and environmentally friendly field of green.

GET SAVVY WITH SUCCULENTS Do the opposite of owning a thirsty lawn and plant a dry garden filled with hardy succulents, boulders, and decorative gravel.

SAY NO-MOW Install no-mow grass to create the green lush look of a lawn without the water and maintenance. Some no-mows are native and available as sod. Try Wildflower Farms Eco-Lawn grass seed, which is a blend of five fine fescue grasses that form a drought-tolerant turf.

FAKE IT If a place for kids and dogs to play is the main function of a space, synthetic lawns are an option. The choices today are not at all like the original fake lawns that potentially contained lead, became very hot, and looked like the stuff lining fruit bins in grocery stores. Today's synthetic lawns are less toxic and more realistic looking, but they are still expensive to install, they don't have climate benefits, and the plastic production uses fossil fuels, emits carbon, and creates microplastics. Synthetic lawns can also negatively impact burrowing insects like solitary bees that need to reach the soil, and they limit food access for soil dwellers like worms. The bottom line is that fake lawns provide zero food for any living creatures, but they do save on water.

Get wild

Swap your time-consuming and resource-wasting lawn for a habitat garden that not only supports local wildlife like bees, birds, and beneficial insects but is also low maintenance, entertaining to observe while relaxing, and full of delicious edibles and flowers for bouquets. You can create a wildlife-friendly habitat garden or make the garden you already have more inviting with these simple actions:

- Add birdfeeders, birdhouses, and a birdbath.
- Avoid using wildlife-harming chemical fertilizers, herbicides, and pesticides.
- Incorporate plants native to your area so they are better adapted and need less attention.
- Go a step further and research native plants that bear fruits, nuts, and seeds for extended visual interest and to feed wildlife.

Top: If you want some usable green carpeting but don't want grass or the maintenance of it, artificial turf is an option.

Above: Instead of buying a birdbath, we added just the right boulder to do the job.

PRO TIP

Consider making your garden a Certified Wildlife Habitat to support local wildlife and inspire sustainable change in your neighborhood. Check out the National Wildlife Federation for tips on how to qualify, including helpful info on adding native plants that attract bees, birds, and butterflies, and water, food, and cover for wildlife. Once your garden qualifies, you will receive a Certified Wildlife Habitat sign to proudly display.

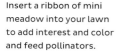
Insert a ribbon of mini meadow into your lawn to add interest and color and feed pollinators.

Meadow mania

For an ecological, cost-effective, and flower-filled garden, create a wildflower meadow in a small, sunny, open patch. Gardening with wildflowers and both ornamental and native grasses attracts a variety of songbirds, pollinators, and butterflies. Creating this type of garden requires knowing which seeds will thrive in your soil type. Wildflowers, like other seeds, appreciate drinks of water, especially to get established, but the surprising news is that most like cruddy soil, so you don't need to worry about fertilizing them.

While there is a bit of time and patience (and weeding) involved as you wait for the plants to get established and become their own low-maintenance ecosystem, the results are worth it. Nature teaches us that meadows make sense horticulturally and visually. Wildflowers create a close-knit community, support each other, and mingle as opposed to standing alone, vulnerable and exposed.

New ground

Instead of turf, plant low-growing ground covers that do many jobs, like fill in bare spots, unify a planting bed, help prevent soil erosion, and provide colors with either bright foliage or flowers. If you need a lot of ground cover, purchase plants in flats instead of solo pots or buy one-gallon plants and divide them up into small sections.

Before planting, thoroughly weed the site and plan on hand weeding until the ground cover establishes. For extremely weedy sites, space the ground cover twice as close as recommended for quicker weed-suppressing action.

Establishing a ground cover requires a near-annoying amount of weeding at the start but the area will be blissfully weed free once the plants fill in.

TOP GROUND COVERS

Berkeley sedge
(*Carex tumulicola*)

Blue star creeper
(*Isotoma fluviatilis*)

Candytuft
(*Iberis sempervirens*)

Carpet bugleweed
(*Ajuga reptans*)

Creeping phlox
(*Phlox stolonifera*)

Elfin thyme
(*Thymus serpyllum*
'Elfin')

Emerald carpet
creeping raspberry
(*Rubus pentalobus*
'Emerald Carpet')

Hardy geranium
(*Geranium* spp.)

Ice plant
(*Delosperma* spp.)

Mondo grass
(*Ophiopogon
japonicus*)

Myoporum
(*Myoporum
parvifolium*)

Sand dune sedge
(*Carex pansa*)

Silver carpet
(*Dymondia
margaretae*)

Sweet flag
(*Acorus gramineus*)

Sweet woodruff
(*Galium odoratum*)

Woolly thyme
(*Thymus
pseudolanuginosus*)

Dry streambeds can provide the tranquility of larger water features without the expense of actual water.

Dry streambed

If you have a low spot in your lawn that always seems soggy and grows more moss than grass, or if you want to change up your lawn area completely, install a dry streambed. This feature is a shallow trench that is lined with permeable landscape fabric and filled with various sizes of stones and boulders. It can act as a drain in rainy weather and evoke the presence of water during dry spells. Adding plants along the edges softens the hard stone materials, enhances a natural look, and creates the illusion of a stream running through your yard.

PART THREE

POPULATING *with* PLANTS

Chapter 7

your PLANT PARTNERS

AH, PLANTS, MY FAVORITE PART OF A GARDEN. PLANTS GIVE YOU flowers, feed birds and pollinators (and, of course, you), can smell heavenly, and can be cut and brought inside to make arrangements. With some early planning, the plants you grow can also serve many benefits to your overall garden, keeping it healthy, robust, and thriving. As much as plants such as annuals can add overnight impact during a garden refresh, planning beyond instant gratification will save money in the long run and keep your yard interesting over several seasons.

Plants are fraught with duality: carefree but fickle, beautiful but devilish. They can play innocent until you turn your back, then they take over the world, or they promise you a full bouquet and at the last second drop their buds leaving you with zilch. Some plants have spikes and thorns that poke you in the thumb when you least expect it or hide

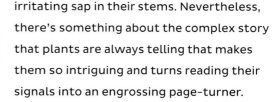

irritating sap in their stems. Nevertheless, there's something about the complex story that plants are always telling that makes them so intriguing and turns reading their signals into an engrossing page-turner.

Opposite: Few things appeal to our wild roots or set the mood of a space as effectively as plants.

Below: Plants tell stories of climate, soil, sun, and serendipity.

A successful garden filled with plant characters is also a mixed-media work of art, a collection of contrasting colors, shapes, patterns, and rhythms. When you're figuring out your design, don't be afraid to act like an artist or designer who works with fabric and color swatches—go to nurseries and pick up and carry around different plants, pairing them on site. See if that pink rose goes nicely with the deep purple verbena. (Just remember to put all plants back in their proper place when you are done.)

Remember also that in addition to form and color, you'll want to pair plants according to need—there's no sense pairing a shade-lover with a sun-worshipper if one is going to wither and die shortly after planting. At its best, a planting design is a multilayered piece where each independent plant depends on its neighbor for support, visual contrast, and harmony. A plant-filled garden should function as a close-knit community, and it's your job to provide a home where all can thrive.

Don't be shy at the nursery. I always bring together my plant options to see how they look in combination before committing.

maximize your plant posse without going broke

Unfortunately, plants can be pricey (and they seem to be getting pricier by the second). If you're like me, you'll visit a nursery, instantly fall in love with a plant and put it in your cart, ignoring the price tag. This kind of impulse buying is a terrible habit, and as much as I can, I try to resist it. I urge you to do the same. One coping mechanism is to plan on one or two in-the-moment purchases, just to satisfy the craving, while making smart choices for the rest. If you follow these basic concepts when you make plant lists and go plant shopping, you will be able to fill your garden with more plants for less money.

Location matters

Have you heard the phrase, "Right plant, right place"? This traditional maxim of successful gardening is worth embracing. The goal is to match your plants to their habitat while keeping in mind that the right spot includes many factors: sun, wind, rain, snow, frost, soil, and microclimate. Think of your garden as an environment where living organisms such as plants, birds, insects, and other animals need to coexist happily with other elements such as the soil and the weather. The goal is to set everybody up for success so your plants can be independent and you don't have to fuss over them so much (although we avid gardeners do love fussing).

With weather unpredictable and climate in flux, it is important to choose plants that match the light, soil, moisture, and nutrients of your garden, which should eliminate the need for a lot of ongoing care. Plants that are comfortable in their location tend to be stronger, more resilient, and better at adapting, and require less staking, watering, feeding, and pest management. While some plants cost more than others, trying to keep the wrong plant alive is more expensive in the long run, and more frustrating.

In other words, if your summers are hot and humid, don't grow plants that prefer shady, cool temperatures. If you live on a hill where the soil is rocky, don't choose plants that love rich, moist soil. Bottom line, don't fight your site. Select plants that thrive in the conditions you have, and you'll be setting yourself and your plants up for success.

Top: The best chance for success with a plant is to pay attention to its label, which states sun and water needs plus its ultimate size. Heuchera, hellebores, and ligularia all thrive in this partly shady garden.

Above: Choosing plants predisposed to growing well on slopes, like aloes and ornamental grasses, results in a lush and beautiful display with minimal fuss and water.

Fit is important

Buying the right size plants for your garden results in them needing less care while they grow. Research the ultimate size of the plants you want to add—the best place to start is the plant tag, which almost always lists ultimate height and width—and take it seriously. I'm almost embarrassed to admit that when I started gardening, I sort of ignored or was in denial of how big certain plants could get. Many huge mistakes taught me that even innocent-looking four-inch pots can hold plants that explode to gigantic proportions. Purchasing plants that fit the size of your garden saves you time and money spent on pruning and potentially having to remove plants that have outgrown their shoes. If you need help visualizing, visit a botanical garden or a friend's yard with mature plantings to get an idea of how large certain plants can become.

Start healthy, stay healthy

Buy healthy plants that show no signs of disease or pests. Playing nursemaid to a sickly plant costs you time and resources, and the ill plant can quickly infect other garden inhabitants. So, play detective and investigate the undersides of the leaves and stems, looking out for spots, suspicious webbing, discolored leaves, or bad bugs such as scale. Also reject wilting, drought-stressed and droopy leaves, as you can't be sure the plant will fully recover. Before planting any nursery-grown plants whose soil and roots appear overly dry, soak the pots in a bucket of water or a filled wheelbarrow. Wait until you don't see any bubbles then remove the plant from the bucket and then from the pot.

Make sure new plants are well hydrated before you plant them.

Top: Healthy lettuce that has not spent too much time in its starter pot and is ready for planting.

Above: Check to see whether a plant, like this one, is root bound before buying it. A congested plant is already under stress and transplanting will exacerbate that.

Look to your roots

Buy well-rooted plants, as those with a strong root structure will recover from transplant shock more quickly. Avoid root-bound plants, as their growth will be slowed and stunted and could even be a death sentence. If you see a mass of roots desperately trying to escape from the pot and clogging the drain holes, if roots circle a pot's walls in a dizzying mess, or if a container looks a bit bulgy like it wants to split at the seams, then say a big "no thank you." These plants are root bound and stressed out and you can do better. Ideally, roots should consume one half to three quarters of the soil in a pot. On the flip side, too few roots may mean the plant was recently transplanted and is too young to plant out.

Foliage first

Before becoming fixated on flowers, remember that uniquely shaped or colored foliage can also produce dramatic, year-round interest. Include plants with a variety of leaf shapes and textures for a dynamic display and more options to complement the flowers you choose.

Keep in mind that cultivating abundant displays of blossoming flowers often requires constant pruning and deadheading. The results of this work are quite rewarding, but it's also nice to have areas of the garden that don't require so much effort to keep everything looking stellar. One win-win situation is to choose blooming plants that also have vibrant foliage, which continue to make an impression even after the flowers fade.

Above left: Some plants, like this canna, pack a double punch of bright blooms and fabulous foliage.

Above: Getting sedum and pennisetum blooms as abundant as these luckily doesn't require excess pruning and deadheading.

Be smart about blooms

If you can bear to resist, don't buy plants that are already blooming excessively. Growers sometimes force plants into bloom to attract buyers, but this can result in a less healthy and less vigorous plant. One or two flowers is enough to let you match the plant tag to the flower color and to reassure you that the plant is not mislabeled. Also, a blooming plant may have reached its peak and be almost done for the season so you won't be able to enjoy those flowers for long. Check the tag to see how long the plant is supposed to be in bloom.

All is as it should be in this properly spaced border. Plants grow. Plants grow. Plants grow.

Remember room to breathe

One of the most common garden mistakes is overplanting. I know it's tempting. But while packing in the petunias will result in an amazingly full garden in the first season, within a year or less, everything will be shoulder to shoulder with no room to breathe, and then disaster could strike. In overcrowded gardens, plants can smother other plants, or tower over their neighbors creating shade. Thanks to root competition and reduced air flow and light, an overcrowded garden is more vulnerable to diseases and pests. Plus, it is so disheartening to watch a design you spent time and effort on become a jungly mess.

Instead of overplanting, try social distancing (you're a pro at that now). When you worry that your garden is looking sparse, repeat three times after me: *plants grow, plants grow, plants grow*. Believe what a plant's tag says about its ultimate size, and take the time to space out plants accordingly. Gardens can easily take two or three years to start to look "grown-in." Think of plants, especially perennials, as an investment in the future, and infill with a few annuals for instant color gratification. Practicing patience will save you money and give plants time to mature and achieve their ideal form. Remember, gardening is a journey, not a destination, and your garden doesn't need to be done all at once.

Repetition brings unity

Using many different types of plants without repetition often results in a garden looking disorganized and messy. The solution is to buy many of the same plant and repeat, repeat, repeat. Repetition, especially of a ground cover, is a designer's best trick for unifying a garden and giving a planting scheme flow, rhythm, and impact. One of our golden rules for borders is to group at least three of the same plant together, and for larger borders five or seven.

Water wisely

Water shortages and droughts are making headlines more and more. As gardeners, we must continually search for ways to make our gardens less thirsty, and one way is to choose low-water, high-impact plants. Cacti and succulents are often people's first thought when it comes to water-wise gardening, but they aren't to everyone's taste and aren't recommended for all climates. Local natives are another good choice, though not all are water-wise.

Many gardeners are gravitating to Mediterranean plants and plants originating from places like New Zealand. These summer-dry plants offer many benefits in addition to drought tolerance—they look lovely, often have intoxicating scents, and go hand in hand with habitat gardening as they attract beneficial bees, insects, butterflies, and hummingbirds. Another bonus: deer despise a lot of these plants, as many attributes designed for conserving water in dry climates, like wooly, oily, highly alkaline, or aromatic leaves, just so happen to make them unappetizing to grazers.

When looking for Mediterranean-climate plants, remember to avoid the dreaded zonal denial. Don't pretend you live in a warmer climate than you really do. Learn your climate zone then find a comparable one in say, Chili, coastal California, southern and southwestern Australia, South Africa, or southwest Europe. The plants that will grow well for you depend on your specific microclimate and site: the degree of slope, amount of coastal fog and drying winds, soil type, and sun exposure. As you look for water-conscious alternatives, always make sure your choices match your site.

Opposite, top to bottom:

A repeating pattern of *Coleonema pulchellum* 'Sunset Gold' gives this border rhythm and helps it feel orderly.

Using one plant several times, like Platinum Beauty lomandra, helps unify a rambunctious border.

Below: Succulents are a go-to choice for water-wise gardening, but summer-dry or Mediterranean might be a better choice for your colder zone.

TOP MEDITERRANEAN PLANTS FOR MANY US ZONES

Agave (*Agave* spp.)

Aloe (*Aloe* spp.)

Cabbage tree
(*Cordyline* spp.)

California lilac
(*Ceanothus* spp.)

Coast rosemary
(*Westringia fruticosa*)

Kangaroo paw
(*Anigozanthos* spp.)

Lavender
(*Lavandula* spp.)

New Zealand flax
(*Phormium* spp.)

Rockrose (*Cistus* spp.)

Rosemary
(*Salvia rosmarinus*)

Salvia (*Salvia* spp.)

Spider flower
(*Grevillea* spp.)

Spurge
(*Euphorbia* spp.)

Yarrow
(*Achillea millefolium*)

Yucca (*Yucca* spp.)

TOP LONG-LIVED PLANTS

Ginkgo
(*Ginkgo biloba*)

Grape (*Vitis* spp.)

Iris (*Iris* spp.)

Lilac
(*Syringa vulgaris*)

Maple (*Acer* spp.)

Old garden roses

TOP QUICK-GROWING PLANTS

Abelia (*Abelia* spp.)

Fountain grass
(*Pennisetum* spp.)

Lantana
(*Lantana* spp.)

Mexican daisy
(*Erigeron
karvinskianus*)

Mexican orange
(*Choisya ternata*)

By choosing drought-tolerant plants that aren't water hogs, you can save time watering while protecting your utility bill. And if you group together plants with the same water needs you'll be able to water even more efficiently.

Bigger isn't better

Buy the smallest size plants you can tolerate for the majority of your plantings. Think four-inch instead of one-gallon and five-gallon instead of fifteen-gallon. This will save you not only the cost of the plant but also the effort to deliver, dig the hole, and plant it.

When you buy a large perennial from a nursery, you're paying for a plant that was nurtured in a perfect environment. Unfortunately, your garden won't offer the same climate-controlled conditions, so it's smarter to start with smaller, younger specimens that will adapt faster to your specific environment.

However, to give your garden an established feeling, consider splurging on a few larger plants. Mature trees offer immediate dramatic impact and structure. If you need to screen a view, fifteen-gallon or larger shrubs are a good initial investment too. In all other cases, keep these points in mind: most smaller trees will catch up with a larger one in a few seasons, survival rate is better for smaller plants because they aren't as affected by transplant stress, and less stress means your plant will confront fewer insect and disease problems.

Balance speed with longevity

Mix fast-growing plants with slower-growing, long-lived plants. Fast growers will give you more immediate gratification in the garden, but the downside is that these quick guys sometimes have a shorter lifespan. To balance this, blend in long-lived plants that stick around year after year.

Water-wise plants perform just as beautifully as those that guzzle water. Some of my favorites include *Acacia cognata* 'Cousin Itt', leucadendrons, and senecios.

PRO TIP

Can you say *free trees* three times fast? The Arbor Day Foundation and many city programs give away trees for free and their choices have been selected because they grow well in your area. An internet search should turn up your best local free-tree options.

Trees have a lot to give

Trees give you a big return on your money—think cooling shade, a strong visual statement, and increased home value—but trying to move a large tree isn't like moving your bed to a different part of your room. Tree removal is expensive and not a guaranteed success, so choose your tree and its final location wisely. Before you plant your tree, make sure the space will allow it to grow to its mature size, and that its crown won't interfere with overhead power lines or its roots with foundations, walkways, sidewalks, or underground pipes or utility lines. Consider planting deciduous trees to shade out the summer sun and let in much-needed winter light. Planting trees that shade the west and east sides of your house can save you money on cooling and heating costs, but avoid planting evergreen trees that will shade south-facing windows because they'll block winter light and increase heating costs.

Planting a tree doesn't just benefit you. A mature tree can ingest forty-eight pounds of carbon dioxide gas per year and emit enough oxygen to support two people. Planting a tree is also an investment in the future. Most smartly chosen and placed trees will only need you to water them for the first year or two. After that they will continue creating beauty, providing shade that naturally cools your house, and increasing your property value year after year, without asking much of you.

Trees offer structure, shade, and beauty while asking little in return.

Plants can look after each other

Companion planting is the practice of creating plant neighborhoods that help one another stay healthy and thrive. Specifically, they repel pests, attract beneficial insects and pollinators, and improve growth, vigor, and the flavor of certain crops. With the plants looking out for one another, the amount of attention you need to devote to your plants is reduced. Plus, having healthy plants means buying fewer replacements over time, which saves you money. While there are many theories and opinions about the best plant combinations, your best bet is to try some out and see what works best for your garden.

Marigolds are a classic companion plant because they repel many pests and attract others, "sacrificing" themselves so your crops don't get gobbled up.

TOP PLANTS FOR NEIGHBORLY LOVE

- French marigolds discourage nematodes and other beasties in the garden bed.
- Large African marigolds protect tomatoes, cucumbers, and squash.
- Nasturtiums attract aphids away from other plants.
- Sunflowers, dill, and fennel planted together control aphids and leaf miners.
- Calendula with beans help keep garden troublemakers away.
- Basil with tomatoes is a double win because basil improves the flavor of tomatoes while also repelling flies and mosquitos.
- Nasturtiums planted with lemon basil deter white flies from tomatoes.
- Garlic, onions, and chives release compounds in the soil that remove soil-borne pests.
- Sage and chives improve the flavor of carrots.
- Marjoram helps everything and repels cabbage moth, so plant some near broccoli.
- Plant rosemary and dill near members of the cabbage family.
- Borage, the babysitter plant, is not only a favorite of bees, it also "nurses" squash, spinach, strawberries, and tomatoes and deters tomato worms.
- Garlic with roses deters aphids and Japanese beetles.
- Tansy under fruit trees deters Japanese beetles and ants.

TOP PLANTS TO LURE AND FEED THE GOOD BUGS

Cosmos
(*Cosmos bipinnatus*)

Dill
(*Anethum graveolens*)

Marigold
(*Tagetes* spp.)

Nasturtium
(*Tropaeolum majus*)

Rosemary
(*Salvia rosmarinus*)

Sage (*Salvia officinalis*)

Sunflower
(*Helianthus annuus*)

Sweet alyssum
(*Lobularia maritima*)

Thyme (*Thymus* spp.)

Yarrow
(*Achillea millefolium*)

know your enemies, feed your guests

At some point, every garden enters a war with bad bugs, but you can retaliate by attracting natural beneficial creatures who are able and willing to prey on the bully bugs for free. Nurseries and online stores now sell ladybugs, praying mantises, and other beneficial bugs

Above: French marigolds bloom for a long time, so they can attract beneficial insects throughout the seasons.

Opposite: Pollinator-friendly calendula and peas are classic companions.

to frustrated gardeners, but these critters in a container are not cheap. Worse, they aren't exactly loyal—just because you brought them home, doesn't mean they'll stay in your garden and hang out doing their thing. The better option is to encourage native populations that already exist in your garden and to add plants that encourage hardworking predatory insects to ride into town and save the day.

For the non-squeamish, hand-picking critters off your vulnerable plants can be a productive option. Slugs, snails, tomato hornworms, and cucumber beetles are all easy to pick off by hand and drown in a bucket of soapy water, as are my big nemesis: curculios that attack innocent roses.

Avoid spraying pesticides. It may kill off undesirables, but your helpful flying and crawling friends will be collateral damage.

Ladybugs and other predatory insects get a lot of press when we talk about making gardens welcoming for wildlife. But these aren't the only visitors you should be rolling out the welcome mat for while designing a garden. Get the amenities right, and you can have a whole battalion of pest-chomping specialists living right outside your door, making you and your garden happy.

Birds

These winged friends eat many bugs and a surprising amount of weed seeds. To make your garden hospitable, make sure to provide birds with clean water that offers a shallow bathing and drinking spot. Make sure the water is moving or that you change it frequently—you want birds, not mosquitos. They'll also be happy to find some protective shelter consisting of shrubbery or trees, a bird house, foraging opportunities, and, of course, some seeds for munching.

Clumps of ornamental grasses are great for giving your garden year-round interest, but they also act as shelter for your feathered friends in winter and foul weather and provide them with nutritious seeds and nesting material in other seasons.

Owls

Although they're elusive, you'd be wise to encourage owls as garden guests. Beyond the magical sounds they create, owls are also excellent hunters. They dine on a smorgasbord of voles, mice, and rats and can help control populations of squirrels and large insects that might wreak havoc on your garden. A backyard owl will coexist with other backyard birds—being nocturnal they keep different hours—and though they have hearty appetites, you don't need to buy birdseed to attract them. The key to getting owls to stick around is the same as for most animals—provide their four basic needs: water, food, shelter, and nesting sites. You can find owl nesting boxes online and at most specialty bird

shops. With owls specifically, you should never use rat poison to take care of a rodent problem; the birds might dine on the poisoned rats and become sick themselves, depriving your whole neighborhood of their beneficial hunting.

Bats

Dracula may have given these creatures a blood-sucking reputation, but these nocturnal, shy, and surprisingly helpful creatures mostly avoid human contact and, despite the other warning often leveled against them, they have a lower incidence of rabies infection than other wild animals. North American bats mainly eat mosquitos, moths, and insects like gnats. They can eat many times their weight in flying insects over the season—some up to 600 pests an hour. If you want bats to roost near your house, consider installing a homemade or store-bought bat house. Situate it up high, preferably in a shaded spot and out of reach from predators. Also provide a clean water source.

Toads and frogs

These bumpy buddies eat many pests, including slugs, grasshoppers, grubs, and cutworms. A single frog can eat over 100 insects in one night. Encourage them to set up house by creating a damp shady spot. A simple log placed over a puddle in a shady corner or a broken clay pot buried halfway in the ground is a fine abode for a toad.

Opposite, top to bottom:

Hanging a variety of feeders in your garden will attract a diverse group of bird visitors.

Nesting boxes are a good way to encourage owls to move into your neighborhood.

Snakes

Snakes help take care of destructive pests like snails. A garter snake lives in my garden, and it mostly hides and thrives under leaf mulch. Occasionally, I spot it sunning on the warm stones of our pathway.

plants for pollinators

Hardworking pollinators such as bees, butterflies, and hummingbirds should be your new best friends. They are part of a balanced, healthy ecosystem and bring action and beauty to your garden. Unfortunately, due to habitat loss exacerbated by widespread industrial farming with herbicide-tolerant corn and soybeans and the accompanying herbicide sprays that kill off all other plants, many pollinator numbers are frighteningly low. Pollinators need our help just like we need theirs. Luckily, there are many creative ways to grow a garden that attracts and feeds our resident hardworking friends.

The absolute top priority when planning any garden should be to avoid using toxic herbicides, pesticides, and insecticides. This also means avoiding plants or seeds treated with nasty neonicotinoids (harmful, widely used insecticides that are systemic, meaning they dissolve in water and get taken up by growing plants, causing them to produce toxic pollen and nectar). Also called neonics, these chemicals are shown to harm the nervous system of bees and other beneficial insects, even at low levels. Ask your local nursery or grower if they use or sell plants treated with neonics. While untreated plants won't save you money outright, you are helping protect important ecosystems, which directly and indirectly benefits both you and your garden.

To create a habitat garden that appeals to both wildlife and people, fill it with plants offering a steady supply of nectar and pollen via continuous blooms that are diverse in height, color, and shape and that provide winter shelter. Grow multiples of these pollinator-friendly plants because a pollinator in search of food will find large masses easier than solo plants and will hang out longer at your buffet.

The variety of flower shapes and colors in this garden, combined with the elaborate insect house, ensures its friendliness to wildlife.

Plants, like people, thrive in diverse communities, so try growing a range of plants to increase biodiversity and provide habitat. A diverse planting scheme naturally lends itself to a more visually interesting space—different textures at varying heights create interest on their own. Even neatnik, formal gardeners can achieve this varied style. Just make sure your space has a strong overall structure (well-defined edges, masses of similar-toned blooms, focal points, and bold planting patterns) and the diverse plantings will look intentional and contained rather than haphazard and messy.

Rich in nectar, this cottage-style planting can look at home even in more formal settings like this contemporary garden.

Hooray for hummingbirds

These shimmery winged creatures are entertaining visitors. Aerial marvels, hummingbirds hover like helicopters and are the only birds that can fly backward and upside down. Most importantly (from your garden's perspective), they also eat aphids, whiteflies, and mosquitos. Hummingbirds have an extremely high metabolism due to their insanely fast wing rate (they can flap from 50 to 200 times a second), so they need to visit hundreds of flowers a day. Here's where you come in. Plant the kinds of flowers hummingbirds love—tubular, scentless, and brightly colored blooms (think red, pink, blue, and orange) containing plenty of nectar. Variety is the key to enticing them. You can also make them feel at home by providing nectar in a hummingbird feeder so they'll always have a source of vital glucose energy.

Two-Ingredient Hummingbird Nectar

INGREDIENTS:

4 parts water

1 part refined white sugar*

*While some of us prefer healthier raw sugars or sugar alternatives like honey, hummingbirds don't. Refined white sugar is the safest option for them.

1. Combine the water and sugar in a pot and bring to a boil until the sugar dissolves.

2. Turn off the heat and let the mixture cool.

3. Fill your hummingbird feeder with the cooled sugar water. Any extra nectar can be stored in the refrigerator for a few days.

4. Place your filled feeder outside in a partly sunny area in a quiet location.

5. Depending on the weather and if your nectar gets a lot of sun (hot nectar spoils more quickly), change the solution every other day and scrub the feeder clean each time you add new liquid. Hummingbirds are susceptible to infections from moldy feeders, so make sure you're not doing more harm than good by leaving your feeder out. Never use bleach to clean your feeder. Instead, use a solution of nine parts water to one part vinegar. Wash your hands after handling the feeder.

Hang a hummingbird feeder in the middle of your garden—birds will sample it as well as the flowers, pollinating as they go.

6. Although the color red is attractive to hummingbirds because it reminds them of yummy nectar-rich flowers, you should never add red dye to your mix. The chemicals can build up in their tiny bodies and harm them. Instead, use a red feeder to lure them in.

TOP PLANTS FOR A HUMMINGBIRD BUFFET

Aloe (*Aloe* spp.)

Beardtongue (*Penstemon* spp.)

California fuchsia (*Epilobium canum*)

Cardinal flower (*Lobelia cardinalis*)

Columbine (*Aquilegia* spp.)

Coral bells (*Heuchera* spp.)

Currant (*Ribes* spp.)

Foxgloves (*Digitalis* spp.)

Hollyhock (*Alcea rosea*)

Hummingbird sage (*Salvia spathacea*)

Lupine (*Lupinus* spp.)

Phlox (*Phlox* spp.)

Red hot poker (*Kniphofia uvaria*)

Scarlet sage (*Salvia splendens*)

Tobacco plant (*Nicotiana* spp.)

Zinnia (*Zinnia* spp.)

TOP POLLINATOR-ATTRACTING PLANTS

Aster (*Aster* spp.)

Borage (*Borago officinalis*)

Cilantro (*Coriandrum sativum*)

Dill (*Anethum graveolens*)

Lavender (*Lavandula* spp.)

Salvia (*Salvia* spp.)

Sunflower (*Helianthus annuus*)

Yarrow (*Achillea millefolium*)

Zinnia (*Zinnia* spp.)

Bees L-O-V-E borage.

Lavender is the bees' knees for bees.

Bee good

As most gardeners know, bee populations are tragically dwindling as habitat loss and the overuse of insecticides shrinks their inventory of flowers. To help our bee friends, plant a bee sanctuary. They will thank you by pollinating your flowers, and, in the end, you'll receive a bountiful harvest of whatever you've planted. Like any creatures, bees need the essentials to feel at home: food, water, and shelter.

Plan to grow at least three different types of flowers that bloom in different seasons so bees have a consistent source of food options. Choose single-flower blooms rather than double-flower blooms. Even though the double ones may be showier, they produce less nectar, and the layered structure makes it tricky for bees to access the pollen. Keep in mind that shrubs and flowers found in garden centers aren't always beneficial for bees. Highly hybridized plants have been bred to not go to seed, so they don't produce sufficient pollen or nectar for hungry bees. Finally, did you know that bees can't see the color red? Save red flowers for the hummingbirds—bees' favorite colors are violet, blue, purple, and yellow.

While they're busying themselves about your garden, bees get thirsty. Build a bee bath to provide them with fresh, clean water. Simply fill a shallow glass or ceramic dish with water then add pebbles for your buzzy friends to land on and drink safely. Change the water daily and clean the dish weekly.

Many bees are solitary and don't live in hives. Over 70 percent of bees nest underground—these require bare soil to dig in so be sure to leave some protected, mulch-free spots in the garden where they can make homes. Others, like mason bees, lay their eggs in reeds and hollow stems, so these will appreciate a simple bee house.

TOP PLANTS FOR A BEE BUFFET

Aster (*Aster* spp.)

Bee balm (*Monarda didyma*)

Borage (*Borago officinalis*)

Calendula (*Calendula officinalis*)

California lilac (*Ceanothus* spp.)

Catmint (*Nepeta* spp.)

Cosmos (*Cosmos bipinnatus*)

Lavender (*Lavandula* spp.)

Pineapple guava (*Acca sellowiana*)

Purple coneflower (*Echinacea purpurea*)

Rosemary (*Salvia rosmarinus*)

Many Mediterranean plants like tithonia are butterfly favorites.

Beautify with butterflies

Sadly, many fragile butterfly populations are at risk and nearing extinction. You can help support them by planting nectar-producing flowers for the adult butterflies and host plants for the young caterpillars to feed and grow on. Remember that butterflies are heat-seekers, so choose plants that appreciate sunny spots.

Western monarch butterfly populations are dwindling at frightening rates due to pesticide use, habitat loss, wildfires, and climate change. By planting your local native milkweed for their caterpillars and a variety of nectar plants for the adults, as well as avoiding toxic chemicals in your garden, you can help maintain the monarch migration. Avoid planting nonnative tropical milkweed (*Asclepias curassavica*), as it encourages monarchs to breed and stay in the area instead of migrating to other habitats where they have a better chance of surviving through winter. If you already have this plant in your garden, make sure you cut it down each year.

Opposite, top to bottom:

My crafty husband recycled lumber and bamboo stalks from our garden to make this simple mason bee abode.

Bee balm is easy to grow and will provide nectar for bees all summer long.

TOP PLANTS FOR A BUTTERFLY BUFFET

Cleome (*Cleome* spp.)

Dill (*Anethum graveolens*)

Fennel (*Foeniculum vulgare*)

Local native milkweed (*Asclepias* spp.)

Host Plants for Caterpillars

Lupine (*Lupinus* spp.)

Nasturtium (*Tropaeolum majus*)

Parsley (*Petroselinum crispum*)

Queen Anne's lace (*Daucus carota*)

Nectar Plants for Butterflies

Aster (*Aster* spp.)

Black sage (*Salvia mellifera*)

California goldenrod (*Solidago californica*)

Lantana (*Lantana* spp.)

Linaria (*Linaria* spp.)

Milkweed (*Asclepias* spp.)

Phlox (*Phlox* spp.)

Purple coneflower (*Echinacea purpurea*)

Purple toadflax (*Linaria purpurea*)

Snapdragon (*Antirrhinum majus*)

Vervain (*Verbena* spp.)

Zinnia (*Zinnia* spp.)

A puddly water source is essential for butterflies to hydrate. Create a puddle-of-mud cocktail from a shallow plate or clay saucer filled with flat pebbles, gravel or sand, some organic compost, and fresh water. Top this off with some ripened fruit (hint: they like mushy bananas) and you've got a permanent puddle that provides visiting butterflies with necessary water and mud minerals, plus a good spot for sipping and socializing. Refill the dish every couple days and refresh every month.

too much of a good thing

We all want carefree, vigorous, and foolproof plants, but some become too much of a good thing. Having a pushy, greedy plant can spell trouble in the garden. Sure, these eager beavers may be fine in tough areas where nothing else will grow, or on treacherous slopes, or in large spaces where they are free to roam, but in smaller gardens they can turn into bullies.

Invasive plants create extra work, as you'll need to battle them constantly to keep them from smothering smaller plants or from climbing into trees. They are time consuming, resource wasting, destructive, and frustrating. And they're not just harmful to your wallet and sanity; when they escape your garden, invasive plants wreck havoc on the environment by taking over open spaces, pushing out native species, and creating competition for necessary resources like water, sunlight, and soil nutrients.

Typically, invasive plants are resistant to disease, are rapid growers, aren't affected by natural predators, and have many methods of multiplying (seeds, root suckers, or runners). Before planting anything, it's a good idea to check with your local and global resources to see if the plant you want is on the invasive plant watch list. Some plants on many local do-not-plant lists are still commonly sold at nurseries.

Opposite and above:

Vervain (*Verbena lilacina* 'De La Mina') and linaria (*Linaria purpurea*) are favorites of many butterflies, and both make charming cut flowers.

So how do you say bye-bye to bullies? The first defense against invasive plants is to not plant them. But let's say you have inherited some tyrants. Luckily, there are many ways to remove or contain them—these include hoeing, weed whacking, manually pulling, mowing, tarping, and mulching. Notice I did not list toxic herbicides as an option. Even against invasive tyrants, these chemicals do more harm than good, and they will continue doing harm long after your target plants are gone, persisting in the soil for years after you apply them. Research whether your intruder reproduces by seed or by root, as this will help you determine your removal approach. Usually a combination of methods—and a healthy amount of diligence and patience—will lead to success.

TOP PLANT DO AND DON'T LIST

· DO choose perennials over annuals, as they are a better long-term investment.

· DO a large portion of your planting in fall. The soil is still toasty warm, which encourages establishment of root systems, plus cooler weather means plants need less water.

· DO get those plants in the ground. A sure way to kill a plant is to leave it in its container for too long and forget to water it.

· DON'T blindly trust the labels on containers, as nurseries unintentionally mix up tags. Make sure you're buying the right plant.

· DON'T buy plants that have floppy necks—this means the root growth is weak.

· DON'T experiment with expensive plants if you're a beginner gardener. Instead, make your newbie mistakes with lower-priced perennials and less-costly annuals.

· DON'T keep plants in your garden if they are diseased, unsightly, invasive, poisonous, (especially if you have young kids or nibbling dogs), or in the wrong place. I give you permission to remove struggling plants and replace with more productive ones.

TOP SPACE-INVADER PLANTS

Bog sage
(*Salvia uliginosa*)

English ivy
(*Hedera helix*)

Giant reed grass
(*Arundo donax*)

Golden dead-nettle
(*Lamium galeobdolon*
'Variegatum')

Horsetail
(*Equisetum hyemale*)

Japanese
honeysuckle
(*Lonicera japonica*)

Japanese knotweed
(*Fallopia japonica*)

Mint (*Mentha* spp.)

Pampas grass
(*Cortaderia selloana*)

Periwinkle
(*Vinca minor*)

Pride of Madeira
(*Echium candicans*)

Purple loosestrife
(*Lythrum salicaria*)

Red valerian
(*Centranthus ruber*)

Ribbon grass
(*Phalaris arundinacea*)

Running bamboo

Scotch broom
(*Cytisus scoparius*)

Chapter 8

PLANT PLANS

THE SEEMINGLY ENDLESS ARRAY OF PLANT CHOICES AVAILABLE for your garden can be overwhelming. It helps to go back to your initial plan and remind yourself of your goals for the space. Is it important for you to have cut flowers for making bouquets? Are you primarily hoping to save money on water? This chapter will focus on some specific plant goals and approaches.

When in doubt, look for plants that serve multiple roles. Much like multitasking hardscape elements, some plants give back more than they take in terms of their water or maintenance needs. One way to identify these hardworking members of the plant community is to notice which names pop up again and again on the plant lists in this book. If there's a plant you're interested in that fits one specific need, try cross-referencing it in the index to see if it's on any other lists—if it is, you've got a multitasker and a strong contender for inclusion. To get you started, here's a short list of plants that pull double or triple duty.

· Large-leaved plants like pumpkin and zucchini are edible, but they also make an excellent living mulch that shades the soil, preventing it from drying out while also keeping weeds from sprouting as readily.

· Deep-rooted plants like marigolds and horseradish break up soil and seek out micronutrients that then become available to their shallow-rooted plant neighbors.

· Peas and beans are tasty, but they also fix nitrogen from the air in the soil, making it available for other plants to use for growth.

· Pollinator-magnets like sunflowers and echinacea are essential to sustaining seed and fruit crops, plus they give birds something to snack on in winter.

A well-designed winter garden can be a visual wonderland, such as this grouping that includes *Nandina domestica* 'Firepower', *Festuca glauca* 'Elijah Blue', *Abies lasiocarpa* var. *arizonica* 'Compacta', *Panicum virgatum* 'Northwind', *Erica carnea* f. *aureifolia* 'Foxhollow', *Sedum* 'Matrona', and *Picea pungens* 'Edith'.

toughen up

Plants that are resistant to disease and tolerant or resistant to pests require less work on your part. Selecting these plants goes hand-in-hand with choosing plants that are well-suited to your environment. Native plants are often a good choice because they have usually evolved all the tolerances they need to thrive in your specific area. Also, many common garden plants have been bred and selected for greater pest and disease tolerance. Some plant breeders have created tough new cultivars and they will list these traits on the tag. Improvements in tolerance levels to known plant problems can make it much easier to grow a gorgeous garden.

Not all bouquets have to be made of big, blousy blooms; this dainty arrangement of *Verbena bonariensis*, *Nigella damascena*, clary sage, *Salvia ×jamensis* 'Nachtvlinder', *Centaurea cyanus* 'Black Ball', and *Knautia macedonica* in a green enamel cup is perfectly charming.

flowers for cutting

If you're like me, you love fresh flowers tucked into every room in the house but have trouble stomaching high prices at stores and florists. Luckily, it's not difficult to grow your own flowers for bouquets. I love having a cutting garden because it means I always have flowers on hand, both for my own home and also whenever I want to pick a bunch as a thoughtful gift.

To maximize your cutting garden's potential, don't waste time and money on flowers that look pretty in the garden but droop minutes after being cut. The three qualifications for a worthwhile cut flower are prolific blooms, a long vase life, and easy to arrange. In general, the thicker the petals, the better a bloom will hold up as a cut flower.

PRO TIP

Packets of preservatives from florists make blooms last longer, but if you're assembling your own flower arrangements, consider making your own flower food. A few good splashes of flat lemon soda will do the trick. The lemon lowers the water's pH, making it easier for plants to absorb nutrients from the sugar, which replaces necessary glucose. To keep bacterial growth in check, add a few drops of bleach or a teaspoon or so of gin or vodka to your vase.

Dahlias, like this 'Arabian Nights' cultivar, are popular cut flowers. Combine them with unexpected elements like sedums, blackberries, rose hips, and vines like *Rhodochiton atrosanguineus*.

Another tip is to harvest flowers for bouquets first thing in the morning or last thing at night with sharp, clean garden clippers. Don't use scissors, as they smash the plant's vascular system. Recut the stem at an angle to maximize water intake, strip the lower leaves, and immediately plunge your stems in warm water as this temperature is more easily absorbed than cold or hot. Lastly, change the water daily to lengthen the life of your arrangement.

When arranging your bouquet, remember to look beyond your standard blooms. Many plants in your garden, from herbs to vines, can provide complementary greenery and other elements. For example, the perfect shrub can provide beautiful foliage, flowers, and berries all at once. When you cut branches off a shrub for decorative purposes, remember that you are actually pruning, so be smart about which stems you chose and how much you prune away.

TOP FLOWERS FOR A CUTTING GARDEN

Baby's breath
(*Gypsophila paniculata*)

Calla lily
(*Zantedeschia
aethiopica*)

Conebush
(*Leucadendron* spp.)

Coneflower
(*Rudbeckia* spp.)

Coral bells
(*Heuchera* spp.)

Cosmos
(*Cosmos bipinnatus*)

Dahlia (*Dahlia* spp.)

Flowering quince
(*Chaenomeles speciosa*)

Gerbera daisy
(*Gerbera jamesonii*)

Hydrangea
(*Hydrangea* spp.)

Icelandic poppy
(*Papaver nudicaule*)

Lilac
(*Syringa vulgaris*)

Peruvian lily
(*Alstroemeria* spp.)

Roses (*Rosa* spp.)

Sea holly
(*Eryngium* spp.)

Snapdragon
(*Antirrhinum majus*)

Sunflower
(*Helianthus annuus*)

Tulip (*Tulipa* spp.)

Yarrow
(*Achillea millefolium*)

Zinnia (*Zinnia* spp.)

be smart with succulents

Above: Group succulents together for easier watering, either with an irrigation system or hand watering.

Opposite: Not all arrangements need to focus on flowers. This container grows nontraditional branches and leaves of *Mahonia ×media* 'Winter Sun', *×Heuchera* 'Yellowstone Falls', and *Athyrium filix-femina*, any of which could make unique additions to an arrangement.

If you live in a mild climate where freezing temperatures are rare, embrace the world of attractive, easy, and undemanding cacti and succulents. Succulents are popular because they require little water, are not heavy feeders, take neglect, are generally deer resistant, need little maintenance, and are very photogenic. Cacti are a subcategory in the group of plants known collectively as succulents (all cacti are succulents but not all succulents are cacti). Areoles distinguish the two—without areoles, a succulent is not a cacti. Succulents are native to deserts and other dry habitats, and they have adapted to store water in their fleshy stems, leaves, and paddles to get through dry times. Some are composed of up to 80 percent water, which means they need little irrigation.

In the right setting, succulent foliage can provide interest and bursts of color. But the "right setting" is key. The success of these stalwart beauties isn't immediately guaranteed. Common succulent mistakes include:

PLANTING IN CONTAINERS WITHOUT DRAIN HOLES Roots of succulents will quickly rot if they sit in wet soil for too long.

PLANTING IN THE WRONG SOIL Succulents need fast-draining soil. Remedy heavy soil by adding lava rocks, gravel, or perlite.

PROVIDING THE WRONG LIGHT Most succulents need a good dose of sun to maintain color and shape. Too little sun can spell disaster, but scalding all-day sun can also be too much.

WATERING TOO LITTLE TOO FREQUENTLY Succulents like a deep soaking and then to be left alone to dry out before getting another drink.

WATERING AT THE WRONG TIME The growing season of succulents is during warmer months. They need to take a break when the weather cools down. This generally means reducing or eliminating irrigation in winter.

FORGETTING ABOUT FROST Proper temperature is crucial to a succulent's survival. They generally don't tolerate freezing temperatures. Most are happiest when daytime temperatures are between 70 and 85 degrees Fahrenheit and nighttime temperatures don't go below 50 degrees. If your succulents are frost tender, consider bringing them into a greenhouse or covering them with frost cloth (or an old bed sheet) during cold nights. Just remember to remove the covering in the morning.

Succulents can provide a surprisingly wide range of colors beyond the pale green-blue with which they're most associated. This vibrant pink *Echeveria* 'Afterglow' is a sensational standout.

TOP SUCCULENTS

Aeonium (*Aeonium* spp.)

Agave (*Agave* spp.)

Aloe (*Aloe* spp.)

Echeveria (*Echeveria* spp.)

Hens and chicks (*Sempervivum tectorum*)

Jade (*Crassula ovata*)

Kalanchoe (*Kalanchoe* spp.)

Senecio (*Senecio* spp.)

Stonecrop (*Sedum* spp.)

long-blooming plants

Wandflower (*Gaura lindheimeri*) is a drought-tolerant perennial that will gift you months of beautiful blooms with minimal effort.

Extend the beauty in your garden by choosing plants that bloom for many weeks or even months. Some plants are stellar at blooming with minimal water and deadheading.

TOP LONG-BLOOMING PLANTS

Begonia
(*Begonia* spp.)

Blanket flower
(*Gaillardia ×grandiflora*)

Coneflower
(*Rudbeckia* spp.)

Cranesbill geranium
(*Geranium* spp.)

Peruvian lily
(*Alstroemeria* spp.)

Pincushion flower
(*Scabiosa* spp.)

Purple coneflower
(*Echinacea purpurea*)

Scented geranium
(*Pelargonium* spp.)

Sea thrift
(*Armeria maritima*)

Sweet pea bush
(*Polygala ×dalmaisiana*)

Wandflower
(*Gaura lindheimeri*)

Yarrow
(*Achillea millefolium*)

Favor the four seasons

Your garden shouldn't be a one-trick pony that looks beautiful in early summer and is sulky and blah the rest of the year. The way a garden morphs from season to season is quite magical and should be accounted for, embraced, and even celebrated in your design. Planting for year-round appeal and interest takes forethought and a bit of artistry to orchestrate, but the visual payoff is huge, especially in the doldrums of winter. Luckily, it's not so tricky that you can't manage this goal as a beginner. When in doubt, remember to include the three Bs—berries, bark, and branches—for off-season interest that also provides bird visitors with snacks when food is scarce.

In a small garden, your planting design must work overtime to provide year-round interest as opposed to a large garden where plants can take a backseat and hide. Remember to plan for plants that have visual merit for multiple months.

Plants that hold their berries over winter provide visual interest for you and food for birds during the lean season.

TOP PLANTS FOR FALL AND WINTER INTEREST

Chinese witch hazel
(*Hamamelis mollis*)

Coral bark maple
(*Acer palmatum*
'Sango Kaku')

English primrose
(*Primula vulgaris*)

Harry Lauder's
walking stick
(*Corylus avellana*
'Contorta')

Heavenly bamboo
(*Nandina domestica*)

Hellebore
(*Helleborus* spp.)

Pieris
(*Pieris japonica*)

Purple cyclamen
(*Cyclamen
purpurascens*)

Red-twig dogwood
(*Cornus sericea*)

Snowberry
(*Symphoricarpos* spp.)

Sweet box
(*Sarcococca* spp.)

Violet (*Viola* spp.)

Winter daphne
(*Daphne odora*)

Winter-blooming
bergenia
(*Bergenia crassifolia*)

Yuletide camellia
(*Camellia sasanqua*
'Yuletide')

plant power couples

One way to quickly guarantee a dramatic or beautiful container, border, or even vegetable garden is to find two plants that make a perfect pair. The secret to this matchmaking is to focus on a plant's color, form, or texture, and then boldly contrast but still complement that plant. It's a simple concept but can be tricky to execute, because you also need to think about bloom times, sun or shade exposure, deer resistance, and water needs. Here is a cheat sheet with some of my favorite, easy-to-grow combinations

Dainty garlic chives (*Allium tuberosum*) with boldly veined brassicas

PLANT POWER COUPLES

1. Happy-faced *Viola* 'Irish Molly' with contrasting tones of lettuce

2. Fern-like *Cycas revoluta*, multitoned *Aeonium decorum* 'Sunburst', and fan-like *Chamaerops humilis*

3. The chartruse pom poms of *Crassula elegans* with spiny *Aloe* ×*spinosissima*

4. Pink petticoat-like *Echinacea purpurea* and spoon-shaped *Cotinus coggygria*

5. Flat-topped *Achillea* 'Walther Funcke', cone-like *Kniphofia* 'Alcazar', and friendly *Dahlia* 'Orange Pathfinder'

6. Rambling pink *Geranium* 'Mavis Simp-son' with moody *Heuchera* 'Pewter Moon'

7. Circular *Rosa* 'Harlow Carr' and stately *Salvia nemorosa* 'Amethyst'

8. Delicately flowered *Achillea* 'Feuerland' with generously bold *Hemerocallis* 'Stafford'

9. Salvia and phor-mium with echoing vibrant coral tones

Chapter 9

GROWING *your* GROCERIES

HAVING YOUR OWN FARMER'S MARKET IN YOUR GARDEN IS AMAZING. The ability to grow your own fruits, vegetables, and herbs feels empowering and a bit rebellious. Packaging, transportation, and food storage all require the use of fossil fuels. Did you know that every pound of home-grown produce eliminates two pounds of carbon dioxide that would otherwise be released into the atmosphere? When you have control over the soil, the seeds and starts, and the ongoing care of your produce, you've eliminated a reliance on corporations. You've kind of bucked the system.

I decided to grow more of my own food so I could buy less and avoid unnecessary waste. I felt that intensive commercial farming had limited my choices and driven some of the flavor and possibly nutrition out of certain fruits and vegetables. I wanted crisp apples that didn't taste like a refrigerator. I wanted a better selection of lettuce and carrots. I yearned for slow-bolt arugula. I also secretly thought that if our family grew our own food, my son might actually enjoy eating peas instead of flicking them across the room so the dog could snap them up midair. Now that I've been doing it awhile, I love how infrequently I find myself stuffing grocery bags with fruits and vegetables. And I still get giddy going out to my yard to pick crispy organic lettuce and herbs for my family's dinner or fresh basil to top my son's pizza.

Opposite: Upturned pallets can hold an abundance of kitchen garden crops in a unique, space-saving way.

Below: No boring spring mix here. Growing my own lettuce means experimenting with the tastiest and prettiest varieties.

Don't get me wrong; the process of growing your own food is fraught with mystery, frustration, and disappointment. (Spoiler alert: my son still flicks peas at the dog.) It's a commitment to tending and harvesting. Forget a few days, and the cilantro bolts; ignore the raspberries while they're ripe, and they rot, same with tomatoes. But despite the occasional heartache, the rewards are worth the effort.

When starting an edible garden, many people wonder if it will actually save money on future grocery trips. The truth is, if done right and given time, the promise does live up to the hype. But because the set up can require a substantial investment, this is the perfect example of a project to tackle in stages as your budget allows. Your edibles

will need nutritious soil, so, depending on what you're working with, you may have to buy or build containers or beds. If you are in deer country, you'll have to erect some sort of fencing. And, of course, you need to buy the seeds or plants (although you may be able to get some for free). Fruit trees, in particular, can take a couple seasons to start producing, but of course once they start they will continue for many years.

There's also the visual component to consider. Some people think of vegetable gardens as unruly messes of leaves and rotting produce with little aesthetic appeal. But there's no reason an edible garden can't be orderly, stylish, and productive all at once.

To create an attractive edible garden, start with containers and enclosures that are visually appealing, add colorful flowering plants to the mix, and instead of planting in straight rows divided by blank areas of soil, try planting in tighter groups or in bold blocks for a lush modern look.

Top: Neatly planted Corten steel containers give this vegetable garden a sleek, contemporary feel.

Above: Raised beds look extra graphic and tidy when plants are set out in blocks.

Top: Once established, fruit trees will likely give you all the fruit you can consume or preserve—and then some.

Above: Vining edibles can be trained to grow up simple wire trellises or twine.

If you're planning to build a traditional raised bed, choose an appropriate size. A four-foot-by-five-foot square bed is optimal because you can easily reach to the center of the bed without having to crawl in. And don't forget about access paths. Make sure main paths are at least four feet wide to give wheelbarrows ample access.

Short on space? Remember to maximize vertical growing spaces. You can grow a whole grocery store on fences, walls, trellises, or pergolas. Good edible options are cucumbers, grapes, kiwis, squash, and even bush tomatoes.

Choose the site for your edible garden carefully. While there are definite nuances in sun and soil type, most edible plants will grow best if given protection from wind, enriched soil, good drainage, water, and lots of sun.

Avoid putting your vegetable garden in a far-off area in your yard, out of reach of a hose or irrigation system, because you won't be able to water it. Also, don't cram it full of every vegetable you can think of, leaving no room for the plants to mature. Be aware that squash, melon, corn, and pumpkins need space to stretch out. Rotating your crops is another smart idea. This just means planting different things in different spots each year. When you plant the same crop in the same place over and over again, the soil becomes imbalanced, minerals are lost, and pests start to build up because they know where their favorite target is going to be. And finally, respect the sun and its role in growing food. Most vegetables need six to eight hours of direct sun to be productive and healthy. This means finding the sunniest spots to plant your edibles. If your garden isn't quite that sunny, all hope is not lost. Certain plants, especially leafy greens, can still thrive in part sun.

TOP EDIBLE PLANTS
FOR PART SUN

Blueberries	Kale
Calamondin	Kumquat
Chard	Lettuce
Cilantro	Raspberries
Collard greens	

bonus benefits

Getting kids involved in gardening can be a powerful teaching tool for subjects like math, science, and reading. Learning firsthand where their food comes from empowers them with knowledge for making healthy food choices for the rest of their lives. And the act of tending plants promotes important life skills like responsibility, kindness, and patience.

A vegetable garden can also benefit other members of your community and provide you with a chance to give back. At some point, you will grow too much of one plant, or you'll get sick of eating pesto (hard to imagine, I know, but it can happen), so remember to pack up a basket and share the wealth. Bring your bounty to your neighbors or leave it out on your curb with a free sign. You might also consider growing an extra row of plants specifically for donating to your local food bank. Call ahead and see what's normally in short supply and grow some if your skills and space allow. Look for programs like Plant A Row, managed by GardenComm, which is set up to help gardeners navigate food collection systems.

Above: Louisa tries making more tomatoes by planting the entire fruit.

Left: Extra bounty? Meet and befriend your neighbors by leaving some tasty produce in a simple free farm stand on your curb.

tasty and prolific fruits and vegetables

Some fruits and vegetables offer the perfect combination for bargain hunters: they're inexpensive to buy, produce a lot, and don't take much time to cultivate.

Tomatoes

Most tomato plants will produce at least eight pounds of fruit in a season. Of course, your yield will depend on your growing zone and other climate conditions. It's a good idea to check with local nurseries or other local resources to see which varieties will perform best in your area. If you've got a long growing season, your options may be limitless, but if, like me, your season is relatively short, you want to make sure you're growing varieties that ripen more quickly.

In some local nurseries where I live, tomatoes are the top-selling plant, which is strange because our climate is not particularly suited for them. Perhaps it's nostalgia, but a short growing season isn't going to stop us. I mainly plant tomatoes originating from cold climates; they perform better in the cool Bay Area climate because they're bred for a short growing season. Anyone in a similar climate to mine, zone 9 to 10, should also investigate Siberian tomatoes, which tolerate cool conditions and have a shorter growing season (sixty to seventy days). Stupice is another good option—it's a small, red globe tomato, originally from Czechoslovakia, valued for its early maturity and sweet taste. This variety will give you lots of fruits per plant, grows well in cooler climates, and only takes fifty-five days to grow and ripen.

Zucchini and summer squash

Slightly less productive than tomatoes, these plants still offer a long growing season and frequent crops. Best of all, you can freeze zucchini and squash to use months down the road, meaning none of your hard work goes to waste and you'll have delicious homemade veggies late into the season. Zucchini, in particular, is great because you can make it into both savory and sweet dishes.

The routine for lettuce is simple: harvest, plant, harvest, plant. Repeat.

Leaf lettuce

For sheer volume, you can't beat lettuce. You can eat salad for lunch and dinner, and one plant will typically produce a new harvest every two weeks. Seeds cost less than three dollars, and from one packet you can get enough to make a daily salad for more than a week.

Lettuce can also serve as a living mulch in your vegetable garden—its leaves create a canopy that shades out opportunistic weeds, plus it looks tidy and saves space. Plant a variety of lettuce under crops like cauliflower and broccoli or trellised plants like pole beans or tomatoes to benefit from the shade.

Green beans

Plant green beans in spring, after the danger of frost has passed, and situate them in a sunny spot. Try growing them on a fence line or homemade trellis. Plants yield dozens of beans, and they make a hearty side dish.

Berries

Not only are berries a versatile superfood, but berry plants are relatively low maintenance. Best of all, you will recoup your investment quickly because, while berries are expensive to buy in stores and markets, the plants are inexpensive and they grow fast. Buy bare-root berry plants in winter, as they are less expensive than the potted plants available in spring and summer. Plus, you'll get a jump start on your berry-growing season. You can also propagate free plants from cuttings or by transplanting runners. Strawberries, blackberries, and raspberries are the fastest growers and will give you a crop before you know it.

Berries are inexpensive to grow but expensive to buy at grocery stores or farmers markets.

herbs

Seriously, everyone has space to grow some herbs. We're talking just a few in a pot on a terrace or in a window box or mixed into borders. These plants are some of the most rewarding, tasty, healthy, and trouble-free plants out there.

Herb gardens descend to us from Greek and Roman kitchen gardens and from ancient physic gardens with the intent to heal. Today's herb gardens are just as likely to mimic medieval woodcut patterns with their structured geometry as they are to cut loose a little and weave through perennial beds and vegetables in an edible, aromatic dance. Using herbs in fresh ways adds both style and function to your garden.

Many herbs lure pollinators and beneficial insects who are critical to the health and production of fruit, flowers, and vegetables, and some have other benefits, like basil's shoo-fly powers or how lemon balm rubbed on the skin deters mosquitos. When thinking about adding herbs to your garden design, think beyond traditional low mounding herbs. Many dramatic

Opposite, clockwise from top left:

Taller herbs like hyssop, add interest to a border while attracting pollinators.

Herbs don't have to be relegated to an herb-only garden bed; here golden oregano mingles with similar-toned Shasta daisy 'Goldfinch' and pinkalicious echinacea.

French thyme creeps attractively among rocks or pathways to soften hard edges.

Rambling rosemary grows quickly and helps a garden look fuller in a single growing season.

and stately options like licoricey anise hyssop, hummingbird-magnet pineapple sage, or fresh-tasting lemon verbena can be woven into your perennial beds. In fact, some herb foliage can be visually striking, like variegated thyme, purple fennel, and two-toned sage. Combining different varieties of the same plant can be an effective and inexpensive way to add color to a border, and creeping rosemary and French thyme help soften hard edges when they are allowed to spill and trail over walls, rocks, or containers. As a bonus, herbs often grow quickly, helping your garden look more established sooner.

Tips for growing herbs

As a child, I always wondered why my dad got out the paint-splattered ladder, propped it up in our hallway, and climbed up into our cramped attic. I thought only rats hung out up there, and I couldn't understand why a six-foot-four man would want to join rodents in a three-foot-tall space. Being the curious type, I ventured up the ladder while my dad busied himself up there. I didn't find any rats cavorting, but I did see rows of vibrant green, earthy-smelling plants growing happily under jerry-rigged grow lights. When I asked my dad what he was doing he told me candidly, "I'm growing herbs."

Needless to say, my introduction to herbs (and my father's secret hobby) was quite auspicious. But thanks to my mother being a gardener in the traditional sense, I quickly learned the difference between Dad's herbs and the kind we generally used in the kitchen.

Today, herbs—of the culinary type—are some of my favorite plants to grow, because they aren't fussy or thirsty and they thrive without fertilizer. In fact, most herbs are sensitive to over-feeding, and large, lush herbs heavily fed with synthetic fertilizers contain less of the healthy essential oils that are part of their appeal. Once herbs are harvested, their flavor, texture, and essential oil content wanes, so store-bought bunches might not be as delicious or healthy as you were hoping. One of my favorite benefits of growing my own herbs is that I can pick just as much as I need, which means that after preparing a recipe calling for a single tablespoon, I don't have to watch the remainder of an expensive purchase wither away in my fridge.

Multiple varieties of sage create a colorful and graphic herbaceous border.

The best way to care for herbs is to give them some organic compost or slow-releasing but high-powered alfalfa meal at planting time. Normally known as livestock feed, alfalfa meal adds nitrogen and micronutrients to the soil and contains a natural fatty-acid growth stimulant called triacontanol that revs up healthy roots and stems (roses and tomatoes also love this meal). If, despite your initial feeding, your herbs look jaundiced and anemic midseason, give them a fish emulsion cocktail. Simply mix a few shots of liquid fish emulsion into your watering can to feed them.

You can usually purchase herb seed packets for around a dollar at your local garden center. However, for woodier shrubs like rosemary, sage, and thyme, I recommend buying starts because the seeds can be hard to get going. Most herbs have a Mediterranean origin, so they prefer a good dose of sun and fast-draining soil. They also love a gravel or coarse-sand mulch that won't hold on to moisture and are good plant choices for windy spots. Still not sure what herbs to plant where? Here's a place to start:

- **Hot and dry spot:** plant oregano, rosemary, and sage
- **Damp soil:** plant mint, watercress, chives, and feverfew
- **Rich, moist soil:** plant parsley and basil

Some herbs, especially the woody ones like rosemary, sage, and thyme, are perennials that grow year round; others are annuals that must be planted every year. Then there are annuals that will take charge and do their own replanting—which saves you time and the cost of having to buy seeds or starts again. To get this benefit, let your herb crops go to seed, avoid pruning them in fall, and hold off on turning your soil until spring to give the seeds a chance to germinate.

Unique herbs to try

CHERVIL One of Julia Child's favorite herbs, chervil is used liberally in classic French dishes. It's also sometimes known as French parsley (regular parsley can be substituted in a pinch, but know that parsley has an aggressive green flavor and chervil is milder and anise flavored).

MARJORAM My mom taught me about marjoram as an interesting substitute for its more popular relative oregano. Marjoram has sweetly spicy notes of pine and citrus, making it a particularly nice match with citrus.

SAVORY Summer savory is a delicate annual herb that's a little bit lemony, smells sort of like thyme, and is a characteristic ingredient of herbes de Provence. Hardier winter savory has a slightly more bitter flavor.

LEMON VERBENA Yes, this frost-tender herb tastes like lemon. It's a nice way to add a touch of citrus flavor to all kinds of recipes and cocktails when you don't want to use the actual fruit, or when you want to enhance a citrus flavor. Lemon verbena is often added to tea blends to give them a lemony zing.

Top: Chervil looks like parsley but has a milder and anise-like flavor.

Above: Savory is a tasty addition to the usual Mediterranean mix.

Maximize your herbs (and your hard work)

Your garden will likely produce more herbs than you could possibly use. Instead of letting your hard work go to waste, preserve your crop and save it for a time when fresh herbs are hard to come by. Herbs preserved at home will have much more flavor than anything bought in stores.

DRYING After cutting some fresh sprigs, rinse the herbs to remove dirt or hitchhiking bugs, towel dry them or give them a ride in your salad spinner, tie them in a bundle with twist ties or kitchen twine, and finally hang them upside down in a cool, dry place out of direct sunlight.

While oven-drying herbs is faster, some people claim heat can damage the precious oils. A bundle of air-dried herbs should be brittle to the touch in about a week and ready to be placed in clean, dry jars. The best herbs for drying are sage, rosemary, thyme, and oregano.

FREEZING Simply wash and dry your herbs, strip away any woody bits, then chop the leaves up nice and fine. In a bowl or large measuring cup, add one-third cup of olive oil for every two cups of leaves. For the same amount of leaves, you could also blend in a half cup of softened butter. Scrape the mixture into ice cube trays, then cover and freeze. Once frozen, remove your herb cubes and store them in a freezer bag. These are great for adding to any recipe that calls for olive oil or butter.

HERB HARVEST TIPS

- Harvest basil after flower buds have formed but before they open.

- Harvest cilantro while leaves are small. Don't despair if your cilantro bolts (flowers); the blooms are edible and can be added to salads.

- Arugula is less bitter before it bolts, but its flowers are also edible and add a pleasant peppery kick to salads.

- Sage is better dried for peak flavor.

- Keep cut herbs fresh by putting them in a glass with enough water to submerge the stems (making sure no leaves are touching the water) and change the water daily. Herbs can live on the counter for a few days.

TOP PRODUCTIVE AND COST-SAVING HERBS

Chives	Mint	Rosemary
Lavender	Oregano	Sage
Lemon balm	Parsley	Thyme

TOP RESEEDING HERBS

Borage	Chives	Dill
Calendula	Cilantro	Summer savory

Chapter 10

MAKING (*and* SAVING) PLANTS

GARDENING CAN GET PRICEY IF YOU BUY ALL YOUR PLANTS FROM nurseries as starts or in gallon pots. But if you learn where to look and how to do a few money-saving garden activities, like starting seeds, regrowing vegetables, swapping plants with neighbors, and dividing, transplanting, and propagating plants, you can fill your garden practically for free.

small but mighty seeds

Opposite: Scabiosa seedheads at their pointy prime.

Below: Saving seeds from your own plants lets you grow more of a plant you already like.

Growing up, I'd be sitting in the backseat of our family car, driving on busy Bay Street in San Francisco, and my resourceful mom would instruct my dad to pull the car over so she could jump out and nab free seeds from a stately patch of hollyhocks. She would dart out and retrieve the tiny seeds, and I would retreat, mortified, to the floor so no one saw me. And whenever we took walks, my mom would collect random seeds from people's yards, botanical gardens, or hiking trails, and when her pockets eventually burst with seeds, she would use mine as overflow parking.

This might just explain why I became that person who bought plants at the nursery and never wanted to handle seeds again. Not to mention the fact that textbook-style seed sowing seemed to fit into the same category as me building my own chairs or sewing my own shirts. Never.

Only until later in life did I find myself engaging in my mom's version of renegade seed collecting (ironically to the mortification of my own child) and over the years (through much trial and error) I have totally come around and found that sowing your own seeds is definitely worth getting your garden gloves dirty for and is quite easy (and doesn't require a table saw or sewing machine).

Growing plants from seed saves you money (no pricey starts), saves you time (no venturing to the nursery; you can easily order seeds online), and you'll have a more interesting variety to choose from. Once you're comfortable with seeds, you can even start saving them from your own plants. This has the dual benefit of keeping money in your wallet while also allowing you to create more of the plants you already know you like and that thrive in your garden. If you're just venturing into the world of seeds, here are some important tips to keep in mind:

· When plantings seeds from packets, pay close attention to the recommended sowing months. While you may get away with sowing too early or too late, winging it is not a reliable method.
· A rule of a green thumb is to plant a seed twice as deep as its width.
· Space your seeds appropriately at planting time, especially tiny ones like radish, carrot, and lettuce seeds; if sown too thickly, you'll have to thin and toss the unwanted sprouts.
· If sowing indoors, place your seed trays or containers in a cool windowsill or greenhouse until germination. After the last frost, ready your seeds for a life outdoors by hardening them off, which means gradually exposing them to outside temperatures so they aren't shocked by a drastic change in environment.

Growing plants from seed is a bit like raising a child; both require patience and offer huge rewards.

I always sow cilantro seeds every few weeks for an extended harvest

If you're starting to save seeds, remember that some plants are open-pollinated, meaning they'll produce offspring with the same characteristics as their parent plant. Seeds from a hybrid plant, meaning those that are crossbred, will usually make sterile seeds that, if they sprout, produce different plants from their parents.

In addition to plants, seeds can produce a mixed bag of emotions, from pride to sheer disappointment, from happiness to despair. You'll probably mess something up and do something wrong and most definitely forget to do something important. Honestly, growing plants from seed feels a little bit like raising a child—without the diapers and frustrating backtalk. Luckily, planting from seed can really be the most cost-effective method to grow plants. Plus, it's pretty darn cool to go from something so tiny that a slight breeze could flitter it away to a mighty plant. Waiting for seeds to germinate and plants to grow is part of the gardener's reward. It's the anticipation of what will (fingers crossed) happen. If you're the impatient type or you're gardening with kids, then the waiting can feel . . . endless. But don't despair, because countless annuals, perennials, herbs, and vegetables germinate quickly from seed.

Some plants are also self-sowers or reseeders, which just means that the seeds they create and drop tend to germinate in new places and create new plants. This, of course, saves you time and money. If you want flowers to self-sow, some will gladly and enthusiastically fulfill your wish, just remember to let some go to seed and hold off on turning your soil until the new seedlings have popped up.

TOP EASIEST AND QUICKEST SEEDS TO DIRECT SOW

Arugula

Beans

Beet

Calendula

Carrot

Chive

Cosmos

Cucumber

Lettuce

Love-in-a-mist

Nasturtium

Poppy

Radish

Spinach

Sunflower

Sweet pea

Zinnia

PRO TIP

Speed up germination by gently scratching the surface of larger seeds on sandpaper (called scari-fication), then soak them in warm water overnight. For smaller seeds, soak them for just a few hours or place them between damp paper towels. These treatments soften the seed coat and help shorten the germination process.

TOP SELF-SOWING FLOWERS

Blanket flower
(*Gaillardia
×grandiflora*)

Calendula
(*Calendula officinalis*)

California poppy
(*Eschscholzia
californica*)

Columbine
(*Aquilegia* spp.)

Cosmos
(*Cosmos bipinnatus*)

Feverfew
(*Tanacetum
parthenium*)

Foxglove
(*Digitalis* spp.)

Hellebore
(*Helleborus* spp.)

Hollyhock
(*Alcea rosea*)

Love-in-a-mist
(*Nigella damascena*)

Rose campion
(*Lychnis coronaria*)

Sea lavender
(*Limonium
platyphyllum*)

Vervain
(*Verbena* spp.)

Wandflower
(*Gaura lindheimeri*)

Zinnia (*Zinnia* spp.)

Above: Cosmos are some of the easiest flowers to grow from seed.

Opposite: Zinnias are reliable self-sowers if you let them go to seed.

transplanting

Do you ever feel like some of your flowery friends aren't situated in the right spot and would look prettier and perhaps thrive somewhere else in your garden? Don't worry—this is the nature of a garden. Transplanting or replanting is an important event in a plant's life—sort of like moving to a different house or away to college—in which a plant is unearthed and moved to a new location. Even the best gardeners make poor plant location choices and sometimes need to shift plants around. Rather than ripping such a plant out and tossing it in the compost, try transplanting it to a location where, based on what you can research about its preferred habitat, it might be happier. Every plant benefits from a slightly different transplant method, but if you master the basics, your plants will be happier for your efforts.

1. Give the root ball of the soon-to-be moved plant a good drink of water.

2. Give the plant a slight trimming so it can focus its energy on regrowing roots. For perennials, trim back about one third.

3. Mark the spot the plant is moving to.

4. Dig a hole around the plant twice as wide as the root ball and at least as deep. The goal is to preserve as many of the important roots as possible.

5. Create a firm, cone-like mound of soil in the center of the hole where your root ball will rest.

6. Water the soil around the cone mound.

7. Carefully lower your plant into the hole, making sure it sits slightly above the soil line as the plant and the soil will naturally settle.

8. Refill the hole with the existing garden soil mixed with some compost and gently pat it down to settle your transplant into bed. You can also add bone meal or a pinch of mycorrhizal fungi to the soil mix to encourage root growth.

9. Avoid roughing up the sides of your root ball too much (with the idea that this encourages roots to spread and grow). Instead, roughen up the sides of your planting hole so that roots can penetrate the soil easily.

10. Last, water your transplant thoroughly and keep a watchful eye on it for a week or so.

PRO TIP

Make your own homemade transplant root tonic by mixing together a weak sugary solution of three tablespoons of plain sugar with two cups of water. Bring this mixture to a boil to dissolve the sugar then turn off the heat and let the liquid cool. Feed this to a post-transplant plant patient to help speed recovery time.

Timing is everything

As a general rule, and for the greatest success, transplant a plant well before it flowers. If, for example, your plant blooms in spring, move it in fall—way before it decorates itself in petals. The other option is to wait until after the plant has finished blooming or producing fruit.

Because of the heat, summertime is the worst season to move plants. If your early-spring bloomer is hardy, move it in fall. Summer-blooming beauties should move in fall too. Basically, fall is generally the best time to transplant, because the weather is cooler and plants have enough time over winter to establish themselves and get ready to endure drying, hot summers.

Newly transplanted plants, even drought-tolerant ones, need to be kept well watered until they acclimate and get settled into their new homes. This is especially important in warm weather. I'm sure you've witnessed a plant sadly droop after being moved—this is the result of a plant suffering from minor transplant shock. It's probably dehydrated because its delicate water-absorbing roots have been (despite our carefulness) injured. But don't worry; strained plants usually perk up after a few days of pampering with water (assuming you transplanted properly, and the plant isn't old, diseased, or sick). To keep transplant shock to a minimum, choose the coolest part of the day, either early morning or late afternoon.

Dividing a clump of grassy hakonechloa to spread the wealth throughout the garden

the great divide

If transplanting saves money, then dividing helps spread the wealth and beauty. Maybe a ground cover is spreading superbly in your garden and you want more of it across the path for continuity. By dividing up a bit of the existing clump and then transplanting, you instantly make more of a good thing.

A gardening lesson I learned from my dad was how to divide and transplant bearded iris. Unfortunately, his method was a bit—how do I say it politely—renegade. My dad would stab apart the fleshy iris rhizomes with a shovel, savagely tear apart the clumps, then "plant" (read: chuck) the innocent corms over his shoulder into the garden and "hope for the best." FYI: this is *not* how to properly divide and transplant.

Dividing plants is the best way to get more of the plants you love for free. If you want to create a new garden bed or refresh an existing one, start by dividing perennials, then plant the divisions in your beds. Some plants are totally willing and able to go through the division process—you just need to know which make good candidates. The division process is actually a necessary part of a productive future for certain plants, like irises, that will slow down or even stop flowering if not divided. Signs that your plant could benefit from dividing include smaller than normal leaves, fewer or no flowers at all, and clumps that are dying in the center. Other plants might not show any of these signs, but they may have outgrown their spaces or begun crowding out a neighbor, and dividing them into smaller sections will help keep them in check.

Dividing plants is relatively simple and easy. First, dig up the plant's root ball or its bulbs. Next, separate out the roots or bulbs. Finally, isolate individual stalks for replanting. A good rule of thumb is to dig four to six inches away from the base of your plant so you'll get plenty of roots, but the process is a little different depending on the roots of the plant.

Politely dividing irises rejuvenates the plant.

Clumpers

Some plants, like daylilies, have fibrous or spreading roots. For these types, dig up the whole clump and, with two hands, gingerly play tug of war to encourage the plant to come apart. If that fails, you can cut the root ball apart. Don't worry about needing fancy tools to divide a plant and successfully cut apart roots—just use an old serrated knife.

If you buy a one-gallon plant with plenty of roots, like this daylily, consider dividing it into three smaller plants to get more for your money.

For bigger, beefier plants like an established clump of ornamental grass, cut the grass back close to the ground and use a sharp shovel or axe to cut the clump in half, then quarters. Remove the parts of the plant that have gone out of bounds or the parts you want to transplant and refill the area with soil. Make sure that each division has some stems, roots, and leaves attached.

Spreaders

Many ground covers, like carpet bugleweed, spread by rooting anyplace their stems touch the ground. Simply cut the stems from the parent, dig up the new little plants, and transplant.

Woody crowns

Some plants, like coral bells, have a woody crown. For these types, dig up the whole plant and gingerly remove some of the soil from the roots. Cut off sections of the crown, making sure each clump has roots and a few leaves, and replant individually. If the central portion is old, just replant the young, outer plantlets.

Timing is everything

Generally, the best time to divide plants is on a cool, cloudy day, preferably in spring or fall. By avoiding the heat of summer, both you and your plants will be less stressed during the process. The ultimate time to divide plants is during the season farthest from when the plant blooms, but know that most of these plants will survive an amateur attempt. Maybe they know you are just trying to help.

TOP PLANTS TO DIVIDE EVERY THIRD YEAR

Agapanthus
(*Agapanthus* spp.)

Bearded iris
(*Iris germanica*)

Coral bells
(*Heuchera* spp.)

Daylily
(*Hemerocallis* spp.)

Hosta (*Hosta* spp.)

Lamb's ears
(*Stachys byzantina*)

Peony (*Paeonia* spp.)

Peruvian lily
(*Alstroemeria* spp.)

Shasta daisy
(*Leucanthemum*
×*superbum*)

Tubers, bulbs, and corms

Some plants produce bulbous underground storage organs—examples include begonia, cyclamen, dahlia, gladiola, and windflower (*Anemone* spp.)—and the method for dividing these plants is a little different. When the plant is either completely dormant or just sprouting, you'll want to carefully dig out a clump and gently pull apart the bulbettes until they separate and you can pot them up. Another method is to slice the tubers into many sections, ensuring each section has at least two eyes (spots where stems will grow). Plant these sections right away and keep the soil moist.

Succulents, like these aeoniums, are usually quite easy to propagate.

more of a good thing

Propagating plants is a smart, crafty, and rewarding way to create a low-cost garden and put yourself more in tune with your plants. My mother, besides being a seed saver, was also a polite plant purloiner, who took random cuttings from friends' gardens and random roadsides. She taught me the art of propagating plants, and I later embraced it because I loved making homemade gifts and being resourceful. It turns out, not only is gifting or swapping plant babies a rewarding project, but when you make a whole new plant from a small piece, it feels like magic and takes your plant parenthood to the next level.

When propagating plants, keep in mind that every plant's growth rate is different, as are the variables involved in the process, such as the humidity levels and temperature in your house, the amount of moisture you give the plant, and the health and vigor of the mother plant. Plus, let's not forget that a bit of luck always affects outcomes in the unpredictable world of plant propagation.

Depending on the plant you choose and how much time and effort you are willing to devote to the project, you'll use one of several techniques. I'll walk you through a few of the easy ones—from rooting a leaf to taking a stem cutting to coaxing roots to grow in water.

Unless propagation is your full-time job, you only need a handful of materials to get started:
· Quality growing medium
· A sharp, sterile knife or pair of sharp, clean clippers
· Small starter pots
· Clear plastic bags, cups, or domes
· Rooting hormone

Homemade Rooting Hormone Recipe

Rooting hormone coaxes root cells to divide and helps a cutting develop strong roots quickly. You can buy it premade or make your own.

INGREDIENTS:

2 cups of water

1 tablespoon of honey
(organic or regular)

Newly formed roots on trimmed succulent stems.

Boil the water in a saucepan. Add the honey to the water and stir the two together until the honey melts. Turn off the heat and cool the solution to room temperature, then put it in a clean container. Dip the end of your cuttings into the mixture and continue the propagating process.

Leaf cuttings

Several herbaceous or woody plants, including many indoor house-plants, can be propagated by leaf cuttings. With this method, a leaf and its stem, or even just a piece of the leaf, are used to create a completely new plant.

Fill your starter pots with a propagating mix, tamp down the soil, and water well. Then cut a full-grown, healthy leaf with a stem from the mother plant, snipping as close to the base of the leaf stalk as possible.

Trim the stem to about an inch long. Dip the bottom end in rooting solution, then insert one half to two thirds of the stem into the soil (leaf tip pointing outward). Gently firm the mix around the stem and patiently wait. Some plants may take at least six weeks to produce new leaves.

PRO TIP

The next time you're at a friend's house and you see a plant you admire, simply ask if you can take a cutting. Wrap the leaf or stem in a damp towel until you get home to preserve moisture.

TOP LEAF-CUTTING CANDIDATES

Begonia
(*Begonia* spp.)

Hens and chicks
(*Sempervivum tectorum*)

Pineapple lilies
(*Eucomis comosa*)

Primrose
(*Primula vulgaris*)

Snake plant
(*Sansevieria trifasciata*)

Stonecrop
(*Sedum* spp.)

Stem cuttings

This is the most popular method for making more herbs, flowers, and other plants (including houseplants) without spending a dime. Plant cuttings are grouped into four categories: softwood, greenwood, semi-hardwood, and hardwood. The mother plant should always be healthy and large enough that removing a few stems won't weaken it.

Choose a healthy top or side stem without flower buds, disease, or pests but with a node (the part of the stem where a leaf is attached—it looks like a knuckle joint). Using a sharp, sterilized knife, make a 45-degree cut to maximize the rooting area just below the node. Cuttings should be about three to five inches long (shorter if the plant is small) and should include the tip of the stem and two or three sets of leaves. Carefully remove the bottom set of leaves so you have a couple inches of bare stem.

Since a cutting can't be fed from its roots (because it doesn't have any), it needs a few leaves so it can continue to make food via photosynthesis. Paradoxically, too many leaves will drain energy away from its hard work of creating new roots. If leaves seem too large in proportion to the stem, simply cut them in half.

Dip the cut end of the stem in rooting solution. Next, make a hole in the soil with a pencil—this allows you to plant the cutting without inadvertently removing any of the solution. Place the stem in your new hole and gently firm the soil around it. If your stem appears weak in the knees, prop it up with a small object like a little rock or some chopsticks. Cover the container with a humidity dome, clear plastic cup, or bag, and place it in an area where it gets bright indirect light. Without a root system, your cutting will dehydrate quickly, so it must live in a high-humidity environment. This is what the dome and daily moisture are for. To increase your cutting survival rate, put several cuttings into one container but spaced far enough apart so the leaves don't touch each other. Clean jars, milk cartons, and plastic soda bottles are great recycled coverings to use as mini greenhouses. Remember to keep the environment moist.

You will know your cutting has successfully rooted when you gently tug on the stem and find some resistance. Once the cuttings have roots, replant them in another container with richer, moist potting soil.

Opposite: Begonias are good leaf-cutting candidates.

Below left: Cuttings need a moist environment in order to root; a plastic bag works wonderfully.

Below: Make sure your clippers are sharp when taking cuttings.

TOP PLANTS FOR SOFTWOOD CUTTINGS

Aster (*Aster* spp.)

Blueberry (*Vaccinium* spp.)

Dogwood (*Cornus* spp.)

Fuchsia (*Fuchsia* spp.)

Hydrangea (*Hydrangea* spp.)

Magnolia (*Magnolia* spp.)

Pink (*Dianthus* spp.)

Rose (*Rosa* spp.)

Rosemary (*Salvia rosmarinus*)

Salvia (*Salvia* spp.)

Smoketree (*Cotinus* spp.)

Vervain (*Verbena* spp.)

TOP GREENWOOD CANDIDATES

Boxwood (*Buxus* spp.)

Camellia (*Camellia* spp.)

Dahlia (*Dahlia* spp.)

Daphne (*Daphne* spp.)

Gardenia (*Gardenia jasminoides*)

Rhododendron (*Rhododendron* spp.)

Scented geranium (*Pelargonium* spp.)

Weigela (*Weigela* spp.)

Wintercreeper (*Euonymus fortunei*)

TOP HARDWOOD CUTTING CANDIDATES

Bougainvillea (*Bougainvillea* spp.)

Boxwood (*Buxus* spp.)

Fig (*Ficus carica*)

Meadowsweet (*Spirea alba*)

Mulberry (*Morus* spp.)

Raspberry (*Rubus* spp.)

Viburnum (*Viburnum* spp.)

SOFTWOOD These cuttings come from fresh new (soft) growth. The best time for this method is in spring or early summer.

GREENWOOD These cuttings come from plants with woody stems but while the growth is still, you guessed it, green. They are best taken in summer before stems fully mature and harden. Keep in mind that greenwood cuttings are slow to root.

SEMIHARDWOOD This method is best done in midsummer to fall and the cuttings are from more mature and tougher plants. Hardwood cuttings should be taken at the end of the growing season.

Figs are hardwoods often propagated via cuttings.

Homemade Soilless Mix for Rooting Cuttings

Instead of buying a premade rooting mix at the store, consider making your own to match the amount you need. Mix one part coconut coir (avoid peat moss) with one part perlite or sterile builder's sand. Add a small amount of water and mix until evenly moist.

Water method

This happens to be my favorite propagation method because it is so easy. You simply place your non-woody stem cuttings in water until roots grow. Watching roots emerge and elongate in the water is simple and fascinating; it feels like you've been granted access to behind the scenes of a plant's growth.

All you need to do is take a three- to four-inch cutting just below a bud, preferably in spring when the plant is actively growing. Strip off any lower leaves and place the stem in a container of cool water in a

Water propagation allows you to watch the fascinating progression of roots emerging. We rooted this African blue basil on our kitchen windowsill.

bright spot out of direct sunlight. Then wait until white roots present themselves. Change the water every other day to prevent bacterial build up. When the roots grow to about one inch, remove from the water and plant in potting soil. If you wait too long (which I have totally done) the roots might not properly acclimate to the soil because they erroneously believe they are now water plants.

TOP PLANTS TO WATER PROPAGATE

Avocado (*Persea americana*)

Basil (*Ocimum basilicum*)

Coleus (*Coleus* spp.)

Lemon verbena (*Aloysia citriodora*)

Mint (*Mentha* spp.)

Sage (*Salvia officinalis*)

Spider plant (*Chlorophytum comosum*)

Spiderwort (*Tradescantia* spp.)

swap party

It's almost an unwritten rule that gardeners love sharing plants (and advice). After dividing your plants or saving seeds, consider hosting a plant swap with family, friends, or neighbors, or look on neighborhood chat boards for existing plant swaps (they usually happen in the spring or fall). At these low-key events, you can bring your own contributions to trade or sell. Remember not to swap diseased plants or plants that come from a bed with excess weeds (and keep an eye out so you don't take any home with you either). If you swap a prolific reseeder or spreader, mark its rambunctious tendencies on a label so the recipient can plant with caution.

PART FOUR

the

NITTY-GRITTY

Chapter 11

WATER WISDOM

GROWING UP, I REMEMBER WATERING OUR GARDEN WITH A HOSE—
a hose that kinked up around every corner, a hose that leaked and squirted
at the connector piece that added on another ten unruly feet, a hose
that dragged over innocent plants, leaving a flattened-flower path of
destruction. We attached one of those old-school metal sprinkler heads
and placed it on the lawn where, after turning on the water, we would
leave it for a bit only to return to move it to a new spot (or run through
it in bathing suits). The inefficient spray would water the concrete, make
muddy puddles in low spots, and sometimes be forgotten. Inevitably,
runoff ensued. I do miss a good sprinkler run-through, but I'm glad those
wasteful watering days are over.

Today, unfortunately, the world is either dealing with too much
water (rising sea levels) or too little (drought conditions). Respecting
this precious resource and using it wisely is a top concern. If you think
about it, most homes are designed to drain water away, which can be
good and bad. Good because the houses are less prone to water damage.
Bad because landscapes that drain water away can become stressed and
gardeners have to over-irrigate. On a bigger front, parched landscapes
lose fire resistance and face an increased risk of drought and flooding.
The issue of water is a tangled web.

This is why extra care should be taken regarding how we deliver water
to our plants and how much. All plants need water. New plantings need
more while they get their roots established, but we also need to consider
long-term watering plans. And not all watering methods are created
equal. Shallow, frequent watering encourages roots to grow near the soil
surface, which makes plants susceptible to drying out during hot

temperatures. A more productive technique is to water less frequently but longer each time, which helps plants form deeper, more resilient roots. Slower watering, in which water gets a chance to hydrate feeder roots and soak into the root ball, is better than a rush of water that will probably create wasteful runoff. The most crucial idea is to water the roots of plants—not the leaves and definitely not the air or pavement.

irrigation systems

Thank goodness for modern gadgetry like automatic irrigation systems. Properly installed irrigation systems are the most effective way to slowly deliver water, giving it enough time to soak in and not run off. Plants watered properly with a drip irrigation system grow more quickly and are more resistant to drought because their roots penetrate farther into the ground. Also, weeds are less of a problem, because the ground isn't wet from overspray. No overhead spray also means no wet leaves, which leads to less fungal disease.

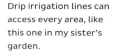

Drip irrigation lines can access every area, like this one in my sister's garden.

Irrigation systems save time and energy, and though they can be expensive to set up, they pay dividends. Definitely consider adding an irrigation system to your wish list, saving up if you need to. You'll most likely want to have your system installed by a licensed professional. Irrigation that doesn't function properly wastes money and resources, plus it can kill plants, cause flooding, create serious drainage problems, and produce excess runoff.

Choose a smart controller to pair with your irrigation system that automatically adjusts your watering schedule to give your garden a customized amount of water based on the weather forecast, the plants, and soil. If you have a large property, a busy schedule, or travel a lot, an automated smart controller is a garden saver.

The optimal time to water is in the morning when temperatures are cooler. You might think nighttime is good because water won't evaporate in the hot air and the plants won't be stressed by the heat, but watering at night means plants may not get a chance to dry completely, which can lead to fungal problems. Another poor time to water is in the middle of the day when temperatures are at their highest, because water could evaporate before it reaches the roots.

Much less expensive than drip irrigation is a soaker hose, which is essentially a porous hose that "leaks" water at a slow and steady rate. In general, large gardens with rows of plants do best with drip irrigation, while soaker hoses work well for small gardens and raised beds.

If you're going old school and using a regular hose, upgrade it by adding a water wand with multiple degrees of water pressure. It delivers targeted water and makes it easy to turn the water off when you need to go back to turn off the spigot.

A soaker hose releases water slow and steady.

PRO TIP

If your soil is dry or you're on a hill, set your smart irrigation system for two shorter cycles to reduce runoff; the first cycle wets the soil and the next cycle allows for proper percolation.

common water problems

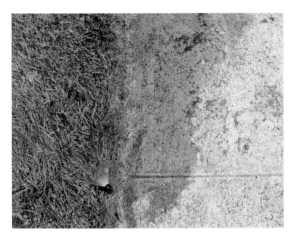

Concrete doesn't need watering. Runoff like this is wasteful.

PROBLEM Overwatering

If you're not paying attention and not seeing the overspray, the puddling, the runoff, the soggy mossy lawn, or noticing leaks in your system, you're wasting water and money and potentially damaging your garden and the wider ecosystem.

SOLUTION Observe and fine tune. Soil type, terrain, types of plants, and whether you have mulch or not all affect how much water your garden needs, so factor these elements into your watering schedule and method. Set your watering system to run when you are home so you can see and hear what is happening.

PROBLEM Not knowing your soil

It's important to remember that soil type affects how much water is needed. For example, clay soil is heavy and soggy in winter and brick hard during summer.

SOLUTION To help plants in clay soil, give them better drainage and work in some sand, small lava rocks, and compost at planting time to allow for more air and better root growth. Remember that plants in clay soil need slow and infrequent watering. Those in sandy soil, on the other hand, need more frequent watering.

PROBLEM Watering too lightly

It is possible to kill your plants with kindness. Know that watering takes time and patience, and shallow watering causes roots to remain on the surface, which makes plants more susceptible to drought damage.

SOLUTION Give your plants deep, infrequent soakings. Also create small soil or mulch basins around larger plants to hold the water longer.

TOP WET SOIL–TOLERANT PLANTS

Abelia (*Abelia* spp.)

Bald cypress (*Taxodium distichum*)

Bergenia (*Bergenia* spp.)

Blueberry (*Vaccinium* spp.)

Calla lily (*Zantedeschia aethiopica*)

Cardinal flower (*Lobelia cardinalis*)

Daylily (*Hemerocallis* spp.)

Douglas iris (*Iris douglasiana*)

Elderberry (*Sambucus* spp.)

False spirea (*Astilbe* spp.)

Foxgloves (*Digitalis* spp.)

Gunnera (*Gunnera* spp.)

Iris (*Iris* spp.)

Mexican orange (*Choisya ternata*)

Red maple (*Acer rubrum*)

River birch (*Betula nigra*)

Shasta daisy (*Leucanthemum ×superbum*)

Southern magnolia (*Magnolia grandiflora*)

Sweet flag (*Acorus gramineus*)

Wild ginger (*Asarum* spp.)

Willow (*Salix* spp.)

PROBLEM Overhead watering

Spraying plants from above is inefficient and unhealthy for plants as wet leaves can lead to fungus and disease.

SOLUTION Water at ground level, being sure to deliver water directly to the roots.

PROBLEM Forgetting about evaporation

Soil loses moisture through evaporation and evaporation wastes water.

SOLUTION Keep the ground mulched or planted with ground covers so less soil surface is exposed. Replace sprinklers with drip irrigation so there is less wet soil surface exposed and water doesn't evaporate as it travels through the air. If you must water with sprayers, avoid watering when it's hot and windy.

rain rain, come again

Rainwater harvesting is the act of collecting runoff from your hardscapes, and it's not just for the hardcore gardener who stresses over every wasted drop. Tap water can contain fluoride, chlorine, and other chemicals or minerals that plants and soil organisms aren't keen on. Rainfall is the preferred drink for plants, especially edibles and potted plants. Plus, it's free.

Passive rainwater harvesting methods include infiltration basins and bioswales that slow or stop runoff from flowing across your land—this allows storm water to infiltrate into the ground, hydrate soil, and recharge aquifers. Active methods such as catching and storing rainwater in barrels or containers for later use also hydrate soils and recharge groundwater, plus you can control when and how the stored water is used. To keep mosquitos and algae from invading and prevent pets and kids getting in, always cover your collection containers, and before you begin with any rain barrel method, check to make sure no municipal or homeowner restrictions exist.

Graywater

The process of reusing household water to irrigate the garden is known as graywater. In California, many people grew up practicing a simple form of pseudo-graywater recycling: placing a bucket or pail on the floor of the shower to catch the water that runs while you're waiting for your shower to heat up. This is smart and easy (I actually still use a bucket in our shower), but we shouldn't stop there. Graywater capture systems often include water from washing machines, showers, bathtubs, and bathroom sinks (but not water from dishwashers or kitchen sinks). Some studies report that anywhere from 50 to 80 percent of household water could be recycled as graywater, creating huge savings, both of water and money. If you're interested in installing a graywater system, make sure to consult reputable resources such as the *San Francisco Graywater Design Manual for Outdoor Irrigation* to get detailed instructions.

With a simple system, graywater should be discharged onto mulch, never directly onto bare ground. Mulch (and mulch basins) can filter the water, allowing it to soak into the soil. Any type of mulch works: wood chips, straw, or bark. Compost is not recommended, because it decomposes too quickly. More complex systems filter graywater so it can be used in graywater-compatible drip irrigation tubing. In these systems, the tubing is used to irrigate a garden the same as in a traditional irrigation system and it can be covered with mulch.

It's a good idea to avoid direct contact with graywater, as it often contains small amounts of bacteria that come from your clothes or body. Don't use graywater in sprinklers due to the risk of inhaling unhealthy organisms. Choose natural biodegradable soaps that break down in the environment and won't harm plants and animals. Stay away from powdered soaps and any cleaners with bleach (chlorine bleach kills soil microorganisms) or sodium and boron, which are harmful to plants and soil.

Graywater must pass slowly through healthy topsoil for natural purification to occur. Before installing a system, check your garden for proper drainage and unsuitable soil. If your soil has too much clay or too much sand, a graywater system might not be a good fit, because you don't want the water to pool up or run off.

Never store graywater for more than twenty-four hours or bacteria will grow, but chances are that you'll have more irrigation needs than available graywater. If this happens, first water large trees, hedges, and large perennials, then fruit trees, and last use the water on edible plants and vines such as corn, grapes, or kiwis where the edible part is off the ground and not in contact with the water. Don't use graywater on root vegetables like carrots, potatoes, or beets, and keep it away from low-growing strawberries, because if they're not properly washed serious health issues could arise.

Unfortunately, graywater can't fill all your watering needs. For starters, it tends to be alkaline, so acid-loving plants like blueberries and azaleas, which are sensitive to salt, struggle with it. Potted plants don't appreciate it either, because their restricted root zones make them vulnerable to damage. Turf grass is made up of hundreds of individual plants and is the most difficult to irrigate with graywater. Smart graywater candidates include clumping bamboo and redwoods, which like the extra moisture.

Chapter *12*

SOIL SAVVY

BEFORE DOING ANY DIGGING AND PLANTING, TAKE A STEP BACK AND
consider your soil. A healthy garden always starts with healthy soil. This
seemingly basic brown material is actually a complex living ecosystem
worthy of reverence—it feeds our plants, provides a space for roots to
grow deep and strong, and helps produce healthy crops, vigorous leaves,
and bouquets of flowers. Rich soil contains a proper balance of nitrogen,
potassium, phosphorus, and other nutrients that support a plant's fruit,
leaf, and root development. Rich soil is also host to dozens of important minerals for growth, and contains the water and oxygen required to
nurture the microscopic animal, plant, and fungi life that helps form this
habitat and keep it in good shape. If there's one thing that pays off for
effort, money, and time, it's understanding and caring for your soil.

to prep or not to prep

A debate is currently circulating among gardeners concerning whether
to prep native soil or not. For centuries, gardeners have created landscapes by adapting their sites to the plants they have chosen to grow.
Now, many hardcore gardeners are questioning this method, believing it
is futile to amend native soil in an attempt to re-create a kind of generic
planting mix that has good structure and is loose and fertile—in essence,
to turn it into something it isn't naturally.

The new school of thought advises against the old practice of assuming you have cruddy soil and hauling in heavy bags of store-bought soil to
replace it. Instead, gardeners are encouraged to analyze their soil, accept

it as it is, top dress with compost, and let the natural mycorrhizae transfer the nutrients into the soil and ultimately the roots of plants. The aim of the no-prep gardener is to grow plants that fancy the type of soil you've got, then leave them to go about enhancing the habitat they naturally crave. Basically, the argument is that it's a losing battle to create an artificial environment in which plants grow where they shouldn't be growing.

I certainly understand the idea of choosing plants that will thrive in the soil you have, even if the soil is not totally desirable, but I think I land somewhere in the middle of this debate. I acknowledge existing soil and realize that not only is it here to stay but also that removing all or some of it is time consuming and wasteful, and starting over with store-bought soil is expensive. On the flip side, rich, ready-to-garden soil seldom occurs in nature. It's certainly rare for me to find it at my clients' houses, because bulldozers have stripped it off the land during construction and sold it to someone else. What's left is soil that feels tired, a bit violated, compacted, and worrisomely nutrient and organism deficient. In these cases, I think it's okay to help soil out a bit, give it a little boost, make it drain better, make it more nutritious, make it so earthworms will flock to it and help aerate it. Plants can't grow if oxygen, water, and nutrients can't make it to their roots, so I like to help them out. I am a mother, after all, and I like to nurture. The perennial question then becomes: how do you boost your soil naturally and make happy plants?

One answer could be, instead of hauling in expensive new dirt, to investigate the soil you have and add productive, less expensive amendments.

Feel things out

Here's a simple and quick exercise to determine the texture of your garden's soil. Take a handful of soil and squeeze it into a ball. Then open your fist. If the soil stays in a ball shape, it's clay. If it falls apart just a bit, it's loam, and if it completely crumbles then it's sandy.

Another trick is digging a hole about a foot deep into your existing soil in the different areas where you'll be planting. Different areas may have different types of soil, so it's important to test them all. Next, fill the holes with water and wait to see what happens. If it takes a few hours for the water to drain away, then you have poor-draining soil and can amend it to make it lighter. If, on the other hand, the water disappears immediately, then your soil is too light and you need to address how to retain more water. Or you could forgo amendments altogether and start looking into plants that can tolerate heavy clay or sandy soil.

Take a test

Unfortunately, soil fertility can't be determined by feel, so you have to rely on chemical analysis. Before randomly adding fertilizers or amendments to fix a problem you may not have, buy a soil pH test kit at your local garden center. If you are the type that geeks out on soil details, check with your county's USDA-based extension service about getting a professional soil test done. For a small fee, they will test your soil, checking the pH, the amount of minerals and nutrients, and the amount of organic matter, and send you a printout of the results. An in-depth test may also be useful if you're concerned about pesticides, herbicides, or heavy metals in your soil.

A test will help you understand if your soil is acidic or alkaline. If pH is too drastic one way or the other, nutrients won't dissolve in water to become available to plant roots. Those plants not compatible with that extreme pH will struggle and stress out.

In general, plants don't like alkaline soil (a pH level above 7.0), preferring a slightly acid soil with a pH of 5.5 to 7, but you might live in an area that is naturally alkaline because of low organic matter. Or your site may have leached lime from concrete work, which can also lower pH. Either way, add acidic materials like compost or pine needles, or choose plants that don't mind this soil type.

Pink petticoat-like *Echinacea purpurea* is a good candidate for alkaline soil.

TOP PLANTS TOLERANT OF ALKALINE SOIL

Aster (*Aster* spp.)

Blanket flower (*Gaillardia* ×*grandiflora*)

California poppy (*Eschscholzia californica*)

Candytuft (*Iberis sempervirens*)

Cape plumbago (*Plumbago auriculata*)

Coast live oak (*Quercus agrifolia*)

Columbine (*Aquilegia* spp.)

Coneflower (*Rudbeckia* spp.)

Fountain grass (*Pennisetum* spp.)

Hydrangea (*Hydrangea* spp.)

Lemon marigold (*Tagetes tenuifolia*)

Maidenhair tree (*Ginkgo biloba*)

Moss Pink (*Phlox subulata*)

Purple coneflower (*Echinacea purpurea*)

Snapdragon (*Antirrhinum majus*)

Winter-blooming bergenia (*Bergenia crassifolia*)

Wormwood (*Artemesia* spp.)

Yarrow (*Achillea millefolium*)

top ways to improve soil

Avoid overzealous digging, walking, and rototilling over wet soil or clay soil. Too much of any of these activities pushes air out and compacts soil structure, which leaves little room for roots to grow or for organisms to breathe. Your options for soil amendments are many, and there's no need to spend a lot of money on them.

All covered

In fall, sow a cover crop (also called green manure) over what would normally be empty winter soil. Cover crops do many jobs: they save you from weeding in the off-season, naturally loosen soil texture, fix nitrogen from the atmosphere into a form plants can use, and add significant organic matter. Classic cover crops include fava beans, vetch, and crimson clover.

Simply sprinkle seeds on the soil surface, gently rake them in, and watch them grow. When they flower in spring (about 50 percent of them), cut them down and chop them into small pieces, then either fork the material into the top layer of soil or leave it on top and cover with compost. Within a few weeks, the plants will break down as earthworms squirm up and nosh on the feast, and soon you can plant your spring garden in your naturally nourished soil.

Make friends with fungus

Mycorrhizae ("fungus root" in Greek) are fungi that create a symbiotic relation with plant roots. These organisms attach to roots and to themselves and send out filaments as much as 200 times farther than the roots they colonize. In return, the plant gives energy to its fungus friends in the form of sugars. Mycorrhizae are good at absorbing water and nutrients, especially phosphorous and nitrogen, and mycorrhizae-associated plants have fewer root diseases and soil pest problems, form stronger roots, and need less water and fertilizer.

Adding mycorrhizae fungi to your garden is a smart way to energize your soil and boost your plants' health and production. Add granular mycorrhizae to each transplant hole at an approximate rate of a quarter teaspoon for a one-gallon plant. Soluble mycorrhizae can be diluted in non-chlorinated water (chlorine kills bacteria and fungus) and used as a soil drench. You can also add some to potting soil to boost microbe activity.

Always check the expiration date on the package of mycorrhizae. You don't want to use an expired product, as you need the fungi to be alive. Store your product in a cool place to keep your helpers happy.

Mad about manure

Nothing says farm life like the smell of cow manure, and, when well aged, the stuff bursts with beneficial properties. Fresh manure, however, is high in ammonia, which can burn plants, and it could be full of weed seeds, so make sure you only use aged manure in your garden. On the flip side, bags of manure from nurseries can be pricey, so if you're able, venture to your nearest farm and see if they will sell or give you some manure for free. Just make sure your chosen farm is organic so you know the manure doesn't contain metals or toxins.

Biochar is an underused charcoal-like soil amendment.

Biochar(ged)

Biochar is a charcoal-like soil amendment consisting of organic matter (wood chips, switchgrass, or agricultural byproducts) that's been heated to temperatures reaching 660 degrees Fahrenheit with little to no oxygen. Biochar is excellent at preserving soil health, increasing soil biodiversity, decreasing the need for fertilizers, improving water absorption, and loosening compacted soil. Plus, creating it reduces carbon dioxide in the atmosphere. You can purchase biochar at select nurseries and stock feed stores, or, you can make your own. For more information check out the International Biochar Initiative.

Whether you buy it or make your own, preparing biochar is a bit involved, but it's not difficult. Before spreading it in your garden, you must "charge" it, which means inoculating it with nutrients and micro- bial life. You do this by combining it with high-quality compost, manure, or worm castings. In a five-gallon bucket, add one part biochar to two parts compost. Fill the rest of the bucket with water and stir. Stir this brew every few days for at least fourteen days and then it's ready to use in your garden.

You can add charged biochar to your potting soil and mix it in by hand or use it as a top dressing and sprinkle it on your soil, but be sure to water it in to prevent it from blowing away. If you're preparing a new bed, gently work the biochar into the soil.

Worship the worm

The lowly earthworm can be a valuable asset to your gar- den soil. These hardworking decomposers will save you from backbreaking digging and aerating of soil. As they move underground, worms constantly ingest then digest organic material. The castings (um, poop) they leave behind make a great balanced fertilizer, excellent at hold- ing water, rich in microbes, and dense in nutrients. In fact, earthworm castings can be ten times as nutrient dense as

Surprisingly charismatic, red wigglers are the worm of choice for ver- micomposting.

the plant materials they ate. The other nifty jobs these natural recyclers achieve through their underground slithering is to move minerals from your subsoil to your topsoil and to loosen the soil's structure, allowing air and water to circulate more freely.

In addition to welcoming worms into borders and beds, some gar- deners embrace vermiculture, the process of cultivating worms (usually red wigglers) in bins or trays where they break down kitchen and garden waste. These worm farmers can then use the nutritious castings as compost in the garden. Worm farm kits are available in various sizes and they don't require much. Important elements are all-day shade (even a shady balcony will do) and moisture. Worms don't like it too hot, so a sunny spot could cook them and dry them out. Kits are smart because they take out the guesswork and help with odor control and proper aeration.

Although worms need to be regularly fed, avoid overfeeding them. They are a bit kid-like, preferring fruits to vegetables, and they will refuse foods they dislike, onions especially. This means making sure some fruit is mixed with the kitchen scraps. Also, worms have tiny mouths, so it takes them longer to eat big chunks of food. If you are a doting worm parent, consider putting your scraps through the blender before feeding your wriggling worm children.

Make sure to draw off the "juice" produced by the worm farm. This keeps the farm from getting too moist and is a free and amazingly rich fertilizer. Add just one cup of this nutrient-dense liquid to a large watering can and give your garden or potted plants a health boost.

Scoop and bag your amendments to save money by purchasing only what you need.

Kids enjoy vermicomposting because worms are fascinating to watch. It's an amazing way to help kids learn about the natural cycle of decomposition and what happens (or should happen) when we throw food "away."

Rock the rock dust

Rock dust is a great way to add trace minerals and micronutrients and to feed beneficial microbes in your soil. Consisting of any kind of mined rock that is ground to a powder, it can also be called rock flour, rock minerals, rock powder, stone dust, and mineral fines. This natural fertilizer is widely used in organic farming. Add a small handful to the planting hole for a small plant and a big handful for a big plant.

caring for compost

Undoubtedly, you've heard of the holy grail of soil amendments: compost. Composting is the method of breaking down organic matter and recycling nutrients to return them to the earth so that you can use the free, superfood end product to improve the quality of your soil.

I'm a big compost supporter, especially when it's homemade. This material is a sort of magic trick, in which you pile up unwanted scraps and, with patience and proper tending, get nutrient-rich soil. Composting is both a science and an art form, and the more you experiment and learn how to make adjustments, the better you will get at the process and the better your end product will be.

Compost also has a positive environmental impact. According to the Environmental Protection Agency (EPA), Americans throw out nearly 40 million tons of food every year. Most of this discarded food is trucked to landfills where it sits and rots in an anaerobic frenzy due to a lack of oxygen. This has irreversible environmental consequences. It takes water and energy to produce food, truck it around to stores, and keep it fresh with refrigeration. When wasted food goes to a landfill, all that (plus the energy it takes to transport the food on that final trip) is wasted. The situation then gets more dire, because as the food rots in heavy, airless heaps, it generates greenhouse gases like methane, which is eighty-four times more potent than carbon dioxide as a heat-trapping gas.

Compost is superfood for soil.

Compost really is a multitasking work-horse. It keeps carbon and methane emissions out of the atmosphere, sequesters carbon in the soil, recycles nutrients, saves water, and saves money because you need to purchase less fertilizer (which is often packaged in plastic, so you're saving that waste too).

Composting also makes you aware of how much waste you actually create. If your goal is to be a no- or low-waste household, recycling your food scraps with a homemade compost system is an excellent place to start.

Compost basics

Before you begin your compost journey, be honest about how much room you have to devote to the process. If you live in an apartment, try a bokashi system. With this compost method, kitchen scraps of all kinds—including meat and dairy products normally banned from aerobic systems—are fermented. This process generates garden-friendly yeast, microbes, and fungi. If you have outdoor space, your options increase. Beginner composters often get hung up on choosing the right style or system. Do you want a plastic tumbler or barrel? Or do you want to go old school and make a simple heap? Each has pros and cons. Heaps are cheap to set up, but more work to maintain, plus curious and hungry critters might be drawn to it. Closed plastic containers like tumblers keep out pests and are simple to operate, but they are an upfront investment. If you're new to composting, start small. Learn how the process works then scale up.

While stringent rules fortunately don't apply for building an outdoor compost pile, a spot in a partly shaded corner is smart so the pile doesn't dry out too quickly. If you want to try hot composting, the optimal size is about three feet deep by three feet high by three feet wide. You could use wood, cinder blocks, recycled pallets, bricks, or old concrete to make an affordable and substantial structure. If you plan to get serious about composting, you might want to consider a system with slats that you can remove to gain access to the contents so you can turn it on a regular basis.

Compost systems with sides and lids create heat quicker, which creates compost quicker.

Turning your compost pile is an important step, as it infuses your pile with oxygen, which the microorganisms that speed decomposition need to do their thing. Plan to turn the pile every five days with a pitchfork. Microorganisms also like moisture, so sprinkle water on the pile after adding materials. You're aiming for the Goldilocks of compost: not too wet, not too dry, just perfectly damp, like a wrung-out sponge.

The basic principle of composting is that you want to combine the correct proportion of carbon-based materials (browns) with nitrogen-based materials (greens) in a sort of lasagna in which the browns are the pasta and the greens are the goodies. Materials higher in nitrogen are green (usually heavy and wet) and those higher in carbon are brown (usually dry and bulky). You need about one part green to two parts brown for a good compost lasagna. If the carbon to nitrogen ratio is too high (excess carbon), then the process slows down. If the carbon to nitrogen ratio is too low (excess nitrogen), then the pile becomes a stinky mess and you begin hating composting.

Don't bother purchasing compost starters. These claim to jumpstart your pile with the decomposing microorganisms it needs, and though they will do that, you can get a jumpstart for much cheaper. Just add some premade compost (store-bought or shared from a friend or neighbor) or alfalfa meal (remember to get it from the feed store, which is cheaper than from the garden store). Alfalfa is high in nitrogen and will heat your new pile quickly. Rabbit feed is made of alfalfa, so their poop pellets are also great for compost—adding not just nitrogen but potassium and phosphorus too.

Below: The more frequently you turn your pile, the quicker the compost will turn into garden gold.

Bottom: Remember to maintain a good balance of browns to greens in your compost.

WHAT TO COMPOST

GREENS
(nitrogen-based)

- Cow, chicken, rabbit, or sheep manure
- Coffee grounds
- Fresh grass clippings
- Alfalfa
- Garden trimmings
- Chopped kitchen scraps
- Houseplant trimmings
- Seaweed

BROWNS
(carbon-based)

- Shredded, dried leaves
- Sawdust
- Hay
- Old mulch
- Straw
- Shredded paper
- Cardboard

Other additions

- Fireplace wood ash
- Tea bags
- Eggshells

WHAT *NOT* TO COMPOST

- Fish, dairy, grease, and meat—not only do these stink, they also attract vermin
- Cat litter
- Dog and cat poop— could contain harmful pathogens and parasites
- Diapers—human waste contains harmful pathogens and parasites
- Rice
- Diseased plants
- "Compostable" plastic—your home compost heap won't get hot enough to break it down
- Large branches
- Poison oak, poison sumac, or black walnut
- Weeds that have gone to seed—the seeds may survive
- Cigarette butts
- Wood treated with wood-preserving chemicals

PRO TIP

Fallen leaves are a valuable resource, so stop throwing them away or stuffing them in the green waste container that gets picked up with your trash and recycling cans. Instead, rake up your leaves, make a pile two feet high, toss straw on top, and wait two months. You'll end up with some amazing worm- and fungi-filled soil. Also, you can use some of the leaves as browns for your compost pile.

Everything you add to your pile will contribute to its nutrient profile—things like banana peels and tea bags will add phosphorus, potassium, and trace minerals. The wider the variety of items you add to your pile, the more complex its collection of nutrients and beneficial organisms will be, but don't get overzealous and add extra grass clippings just because you have them; this overly wet and compacted material can slow aeration and puts a work-stop on microorganism activity.

For the more impatient gardener, hot composting can produce a quicker turnaround than cold composting. For this method, you want your pile to get hot enough that weed seeds and nasty pathogens are killed, but not so scalding that beneficial organisms are destroyed. A happy temperature is between 120 and 170 degrees Fahrenheit. It helps to measure the temperature in the middle of your compost heap regularly, and when your pile begins to cool down, that's when you want to give the mix a good stir, infusing it with air so the microbes can heat it back up again. Avoid being hasty and using your compost when it's hot, as this could burn your plants.

For your plants to benefit from the nutrients in compost, it needs time to break down and make those nutrients available. Depending on the weather, the size of your pile, how small your materials are, and the method you're using, basic garden waste, kitchen scraps, and animal manure can take anywhere from two to six months to transform into

Invest in a thermometer that registers compost heat.

the dark, crumbly material that is useable compost. If you find some residual eggshells and bulky sticks in your final product, don't worry, just add these back to the pile and use the finer stuff.

Compost isn't just for adding to the perennial garden and vegetable beds. Add some to your containers too. All soil needs life in it, and sometimes bagged potting soil is too light and dries out quickly. Compost will improve soil's texture and water-holding abilities while supplying a slow-release dose of nutrients.

When you need copious amounts of soil or compost, buy it in bulk, not in bags, as this is less expensive and eliminates all the non-recyclable plastic that ends up in landfills.

buying soil

Inevitably, you will need to buy soil. Either for your raised beds, to backfill retaining walls, to fill in low areas, or to plant containers. And sometimes you don't have the energy, time, or interest to create your own blend and you just want to buy it ready-made. Though it seems simple, all the soil choices available for purchase can be a bit overwhelming. Your cheapest option is to visit a landscape supply yard where you can read the labels describing what is in the soil mixes and what they can be used for. When you decide what you want, load just the amount you need into bags. The other option is pre-bagged soil from a garden center. Be sure to read the bag labels carefully so you know what the soil is formulated for. The worst thing you could do is buy the wrong type of soil, say succulent mix for your moisture-loving perennial bed.

For pots: potting soil

This light and airy mix is specifically formulated for container gardening, as it allows for adequate drainage and space for roots to grow. Simply add potting soil to pots and then plant directly into it. After a while, soil in pots becomes depleted and can't hold on to water and nutrients anymore, especially as roots begin to dominate. If your plants look a bit tired, aren't thriving, and have lived in a small pot for over a year, the ideal solution is to replace the potting soil.

On the other hand, if your potted plants are healthy but need to be repotted, don't throw out their old potting soil when refreshing them. Instead, break up the chunks of old soil and spread it over flowerbeds or add it to your compost pile. That said, don't do this if disease or pests were an issue, because you don't want to spread any bad fungi, bacteria, or viruses, which can survive in the soil.

HOW MUCH SOIL DO I NEED FOR MY POTS?

16-inch pots hold 1 cubic foot of soil

20-inch pots hold 1.5 cubic feet of soil

24-inch pots hold 2 cubic feet of soil

For garden beds: raised bed mix

This blend is good for filling raised beds that are built atop native soil. Read labels carefully as some should be blended into native soil while others you can plant into directly. If you need soil for a raised edible garden, look for labels with the words *organic vegetable mix* or *organic soil for vegetables and flowers*. Adding compost is a good idea because it enriches and boosts fertility while releasing nutrients over an extended period of time, providing a longer-lasting impact than fast-acting chemical fertilizers.

For fast-draining soil: cactus, palm, and citrus mix

Certain plant types such as succulents, palms, and citrus trees require light, fast-draining soil, so mixes formulated for them ensure good drainage while preventing soil compaction thanks to the bark, sand, and perlite mixed in.

HOMEMADE CACTUS AND SUCCULENT MIX

Mix together one part ground bark, one part sand, one part pumice or lava rock, and one part compost.

An organic raised bed mix is the right fill for vegetable beds like this.

For basic planting: general planting mix

Add this blend to your existing in-ground planting areas.

For filling in low areas: topsoil

Low-grade topsoil is perfect for filling and leveling areas but not great for planting, as it isn't nutrient dense. Higher-grade local topsoil can be used to supplement less-than-ideal native soil if you mix it with compost.

A CAUTIONARY WORD ABOUT PEAT MOSS

Sphagnum peat moss is a wiry, fibrous, natural material that comes from peatlands (unique wetlands that are excellent homes to wildlife and plant species and store about a third of the world's carbon). Gardeners once celebrated peat because it is a natural soil enhancer that helps hold in moisture and nutrients and promotes root growth, but eventually we became aware that peat has many environmental issues. Firstly, peatlands are an important ecosystem that peat mining threatens. Like oil, peat takes many years to form, and there are major concerns over the way it's harvested and how it releases carbon dioxide. Luckily for gardeners, there are peat-free options to choose from, like coconut coir, pine bark, and compost. (There is also some debate about coconut coir's sustainability, as it uses resources that must be processed and transported great distances.)

For those truly on a mission to garden responsibly and sustainably, it's always a good idea to look into how the materials you want to buy are sourced, harvested, and prepared. By choosing alternatives to peat and using peat-free garden products (always read bagged soil labels as peat can be a component in the soil mix), you are choosing a simple yet effective way to make a positive environmental impact and reduce your carbon footprint.

Chapter 13

NOTIONS *and* POTIONS

WHEN FACED WITH THE OPTION, SUGGESTION, OR TEMPTATION to reach for chemicals that "solve" garden problems, reconsider and think of the ramifications. Pesticides, for example, don't discriminate, killing the good bugs that keep your garden in balance. Overuse of synthetic fertilizers releases nitrogen into the atmosphere as nitrous oxide, which contributes to global warming, plus these products acidify the soil, adding high levels of salts that parch your plants and repulse hardworking earthworms. Making and transporting pesticides, chemical fertilizers, and weed killers generates carbon, so by not purchasing these items you are saving the planet from more greenhouse gases.

With any garden, the aim is to foster natural resiliency, not to undermine it and make it dependent on constant maintenance and expensive additives. This is where the creative and solution-seeking gardener enters. The idea is to solve a garden problem without adding more problems and creating a vicious cycle. Nature usually finds a way to stay in balance, and so can we.

If you garden smartly, you won't need to rely on pricey toxic pesticides, harmful herbicides, or synthetic fertilizers. The solution is organic pest control and natural, slow-release fertilizers. Nutrients in organic fertilizers are broken down by microorganisms then released at the needed time, as opposed to synthetics that get washed away because the plant can't use them all or are forced into a plant's vascular system causing rapid, unhealthy growth; when a plant is forced to grow quickly, a multitude of pest and structural problems can occur.

In this chapter, we'll explore simple, economical, and earth-friendly remedies to fertilize, improve soil, destroy weeds, treat pests, and cure garden ailments. Essentially, you will be creating more by using less: less chemicals, less ingredients, and less worry. With common ingredients (many of which you most likely already have in your kitchen) you can whip up a remedy and have it on hand to solve your next inevitable garden crisis.

Double check that your fertilizers and pest-control products are safe for kids and pets.

PRO TIP
If you want to buy premade products, look for the words *safe for kids and pets*, and avoid products containing controversial glyphosate (hint: Roundup).

homemade critter-control recipes

First, some safety guidelines:

· Always wear rubber gloves and a filter mask when applying any solution.

· Test the concoction on a small part of a plant before subjecting the whole plant.

· Wash sprayed plants thoroughly before eating.

· Avoid spraying your plants right before the sun reaches your garden or during the hottest part of the day, as the sun will intensify the material and cause burning (this is especially true when using oil sprays). Instead, feed and treat your plants in the early morning.

· Keep all concoctions safely away from curious pets and children.

· As with all homemade creations, results may vary due to the materials and ingredients you use.

Pulverized-pests remedy

While this idea has been around for a long time and no one knows for sure why it works, the idea is that certain pests aren't keen on feeding on plants covered in their dead friends. I'm no scientist, but I can totally understand this. No doubt the bugs can smell the warning pheromones and smartly stay away. As a bonus, this terrifying odor supposedly attracts beneficial bugs to prey on any pests that don't heed the warning.

The fascinatingly gruesome method is to collect some of the bugs you are trying to get rid of, say slugs and earwigs, and liquefy them in a blender with some water. Strain the solids and dilute with more water then spray on affected plants (both sides of the leaves) to deliver a serious "back off."

I highly recommend you devote the pulverized bug process to a dedicated bug blender (that you could find inexpensively at a thrift store) so you don't contaminate your food with pathogens and, um, bug parts.

Garlic spray keeps the fungus away

Garlic naturally keeps vampires away, and it also works for fungus as a preventative and curative method. Plant garlic bulbs throughout your garden to keep away fungus and provide you with materials to make a garlic spray.

Crush the garlic cloves, add them to a large bowl, and pour about a gallon of boiling water over them. Cover the mixture and let it steep overnight. Strain the liquid and add it to your watering can or sprayer bottle once a week. Spray or water any plants with this garlic mixture to help repel pests. Make sure to coat the bottom of leaves, as pests like to hide and lay eggs there. This mixture can be stored in the refrigerator for roughly five days.

Variations: Add a chopped jalapeno pepper to the steeping mixture or a tablespoon of crushed hot pepper. If you add these spicy repellents, wear protective gloves and eyewear, and keep sprayed plants clear of kids and pets.

Buggy-soap remedy

A simple solution of soap and water will remove bugs from your plants as well as prevent them from taking up residence. Sap-sucking aphids, for example, can colonize plants in no time, especially with the help of ants, but a nice bath with soap and water will take care of mild infestations.

Add three tablespoons of high-suds dish soap to a gallon of water and mix well. Pour into a spray bottle and use on infested plants, taking care to spray both sides of the leaves. The oil-cutting formula of dish soap removes the waxy coating on aphids and other soft-bodied pests, making them vulnerable to dehydration.

Yogurt-spray remedy

I love roses as much as the next gardener, but I detest the black spot and powdery mildew that preys on them. This unsightly condition can afflict other plants too, but luckily there is a natural treatment. I learned about this yogurt remedy from a client of mine who tested the mixture on her roses, had success, and then retested with similar successful results. Now she uses the yogurt mix as an effective preventive measure as well.

Making yogurt spray is like mixing a probiotic cocktail for your plants.

Mix one tablespoon of full-fat plain yogurt with one cup of water, then pour into a spray bottle. After dusk when temperatures are cooler, spray any affected rose leaves. This solution can be sprayed daily as a preventive measure or to treat a current problem.

You can also use the thin, watery liquid that collects at the top of your yogurt (called whey), which is full of healthy microbes. My thought is that the good microbes in the yogurt dominate and eventually win over the harmful organisms. The spray forms a thin layer over the leaf, discouraging disease.

Pest-deterring hair sprinkle

Use hair from your hairbrush or dog comb to ward off invaders. The human and canine scent on the hair can help repel possums, raccoons, cats, and rabbits. Plus, as the hair breaks down, it becomes a nutritious amendment for the soil.

top easy and inexpensive homemade fertilizers

PRO TIP
Don't throw out the fish tank water when you're cleaning it. Instead, use this murky but nitrogen-rich solution to feed your plants as you would with store-bought fish emulsion.

I devour crafty horticulture info like it's homemade peach ice cream, but it's also good to do research and be careful. Some recipes and advice are told so often that it seems they must be true, when really they're old misconceptions that just won't fade. This is the part of gardening that can be exciting and challenging, because what one gardener finds helpful can yield catastrophe for another. Whatever homemade concoctions you read about here or elsewhere are based on experimentation, trial and error, and sometimes luck.

Case in point: one day I told my then ten-year-old son that we were going to do an experiment on our limequat tree because it didn't look healthy—leaves tinted yellow and tiny, emaciated fruit. I told him that what he needed to do to make the tree healthier was to pee on the soil. Well, you can only imagine the joy I brought to this already curious kid. After a month or so with my son frequenting the uncouth urination station, the tree produced the juiciest limequats ever. It turns out, human urine is high in nitrogen, potassium, and phosphorus and acidifies the soil. A French startup is even developing a natural urine-derived fertilizer with the idea of reducing our environmental footprint.

Obviously, there is no recipe or amounts to share, just a story and slightly odd trick to try. Before urine "application," make sure your citrus is well watered.

PRO TIP

Don't drink coffee but want the grounds? Many coffee shops bag up leftover grounds and will happily give them to you for free.

A judicious amount of used coffee grounds make a helpful top dressing.

Coffee grounds for growth

Instead of throwing out your coffee grounds after your morning cup, simply add them to your compost pile or worm bin, or lightly sprinkle the grounds over your soil for added nutrients. Coffee grounds help with drainage and assist in repelling soft-bodied critters because they're naturally sharp and abrasive.

In large-enough doses, however, coffee grounds could harm our canine friends, so if you have an always-hungry pooch, add your grounds to your compost pile instead of using them directly in the garden. Tomatoes and all seedlings aren't big coffee drinkers, so avoid using your grounds on them.

Big-bloom cocktail

After you soak your tired gardening self in a soothing Epsom salt bath, remember that some of your plant friends also benefit from this old-timey ingredient. Epsom salt is inexpensive and easy to use, plus its trace mineral content of magnesium and sulfur can help make plants grow bushier, deter pests, produce more flowers, and increase chlorophyll production. Be smart about application—not every plant likes Epsom salt—sage, lettuce, spinach, peas, and beans aren't fans of the stuff, while roses, tomatoes, and citrus trees love it.

Mix one tablespoon of Epsom salt with a gallon of warm water in a large jar or jug. Give it a shake or a stir, then gently poke holes into the soil a ways from your plants and pour the mixture in. Make up a fresh batch once a month and reapply.

Shake it up

I have a client who swears by literally shaking and ruffling "the feathers" of her plants to wake them up after their winter slumber. I actually do this to my own plants that appear comatose, and while I can't be sure that it works, it makes me feel that I'm potentially facilitating growth, and it doesn't have any downsides.

Homemade tea fertilizers

I am a mega tea drinker, morning, noon, and night. I fancy anything and everything, from a simple cup of peppermint to a more exotic ginger, turmeric, and tulsi brew. And just like me, gardens enjoy a cup of tea to energize and stay healthy. Homemade garden teas have been brewed in the organic gardening world for a long time and with great success. Plants absorb tea nutrients quickly via their roots, gain immunity against diseases thanks to beneficial microorganisms, and produce bigger flowers, tastier vegetables, and greener leaves. Homemade teas are free and fast acting. Use them when your plants need some extra help, or they are newly transplanted or setting buds.

Recipe for Compost Tea

This multipurpose liquid fertilizer is bursting with beneficial microorganisms that benefit all types of plants. It can help reduce foliar and fungal diseases too.

The quality of your compost tea depends on the quality of your compost. If your backyard compost isn't ready yet, it's okay to buy a bag of organic compost at the garden center and use that to brew some tea.

INGREDIENTS:

1 old cotton pillowcase

1 part finished compost

6 parts rainwater or dechlorinated water*

1 five-gallon bucket with a lid (this keeps mosquitos from making it a breeding ground)

Use rainwater or dechlorinated water in these so the important microbes living in the compost aren't harmed by the harsh chlorine and other contaminants. An easy way to dechlorinate water is to leave it outside for 24 hours in the sun so the chlorine naturally off-gasses.

Making compost tea requires a few basic supplies, but the process is simple.

1. Place your pillowcase in the bucket and turn the ends over the bucket edge. Add your compost, then the water, and give the solids and the liquids a gentle stir to blend. Cover your tea with the lid and let it brew for one week, mixing it a few times. At the end of the week, make sure your liquid isn't stinky.

2. Remove the lid, grab the ends of your pillowcase, and lift it out of the bucket. Press the liquid out of the pillowcase and spread the compost around the garden or add it back to your compost pile. The liquid can now be diluted (one part tea to ten parts water). Add this brew to a watering can or sprayer. Use the tea all at once and don't store any leftovers.

Recipe for Weed and Yard-Trimming Tea

Using your own weeds, grass, and garden trimmings to make a natural fertilizer sounds a little crazy, but it is the ultimate in recycling. It saves you from having to use your precious compost as a tea ingredient, plus weeds are full of goodness absorbed from your soil, so it's a full-circle method that extracts water-soluble nutrients and gives them back to your garden. You'll get a variety of soil-enriching nutrients depending on the type of garden material you use. Comfrey is high in potassium, phosphorus, magnesium, and an assortment of trace minerals. Horsetail is high in silica, iron, and potassium because it is a deep-rooted weed that pulls nutrients from far below the soil. Dandelions are rich in vitamin A and C plus calcium and potassium. Fresh grass clippings burst with nitrogen and potassium. Just remember not to use weeds treated with herbicides or other chemicals.

INGREDIENTS:

1 old cotton pillowcase

Weed and yard trimmings, including mowed grass

1 five-gallon bucket

Rainwater or dechlorinated water

1. Place your pillowcase in the bucket and turn the ends over the bucket edge.

2. Take fresh, chopped weeds or yard trimmings from the garden and place them in the pillowcase up to the top.

3. Fill the bucket a few inches from the top with water.

4. Cover the bucket, stir every few days, and let it brew for two to four weeks.

5. Lift the pillowcase out of the bucket. Use the tea right away, either at full strength or diluted, on your plant's roots. The pillowcase conveniently strains the liquid so no troublesome weed seeds enter your garden.

Recipe for Alfalfa Tea

Alfalfa is high in nitrogen, vitamins, and minerals, which makes it great as a natural fertilizer. It also contains the growth hormone triacontanol, which seedlings appreciate. The American Rose Society supports alfalfa tea for roses and perennials.

INGREDIENTS:

½ cup alfalfa meal

1 five-gallon bucket with a lid

1 gallon rainwater or dechlorinated water

1. Add the alfalfa meal to the bucket and add the water.
2. Mix all ingredients together and put the lid on.
3. Stir at least once a day and let the tea steep and ferment in the sun for thirty-six hours to allow the brew to produce beneficial bacteria. The tea is ready when the solids settle and the liquid smells like fresh hay. Add the solids to your compost pile.
4. Use this fertilizing tea weekly as a foliar spray or watered into the soil.

Recipe for Kelp-Kicker Tea

Rich in trace minerals that are missing or low in most fertilizers, kelp is a power seaweed that is helpful to plants when stressed, like during planting, transplanting, and fruit and flower production.

INGREDIENTS:

1 large non-metal container

8 ounces dried kelp

1 gallon rainwater or dechlorinated water

1. Pour dried kelp into a large container. Add the water and stir. Cover with a cloth and let sit outside in a warm place for a month, stirring every week.
2. When the solution is free from the smell of ammonia, you can dilute it (one part tea to ten parts water) and spray on the leaves of plants. Direct spraying on leaves results in a quicker absorption of nutrients.

Chapter 14

WHEN TIME *is* MONEY

I LIVE THE CLASSIC "THE COBBLER'S CHILDREN HAVE NO SHOES" scenario—basically, I'm a landscape designer who barely has time to tend to my own garden because I work on other people's. Because of this unintentional irony, I try to keep a very easy, unfussy, and unthirsty garden that is loaded with propagated succulents, evergreens, and drought-tolerant plants. In my clients' gardens, I'm constantly reminded that some plants need more attention than others—they grow faster and demand more light, water, and food. And when you don't pay attention, the plants can pout, sulk, and throw hissy fits, and the garden space stops looking well tended and appealing and reverts to an unsightly mess.

It's important to remember that a garden is never finished or complete—there is no end product. There is no putting your feet up on the fancy new ottoman and calling it a day, because, unlike the footrest that just sits there on your floor, even a well-pruned shrub doesn't stop growing. But that is the real beauty and wonder and excitement (and sometimes overwhelming and exhausting) aspect of gardening. There is always something to do.

When you find the time to tackle garden chores, you want to be efficient and productive, spending the least amount of time but producing maximum results, because, soon enough, it will be time to prune that rose bush again. As my family says, "Work smarter, not harder."

The more water-wise and low-maintenance plants you include in your garden, the more time you can spend simply enjoying it.

garden chores for every season

Just like plants, some chores are seasonal and some are evergreen. These are tasks you should do year round for garden success.

Patrol

Routinely walk through your garden keeping an eye out for pests, diseases, or wilting leaves. If you notice trouble early on and prevent problems before they start, you save yourself a lot of work.

Record

Start a phenology journal to track insects, weather, bird populations, and fruiting and flowering times in the garden. Also write down plant varieties worth remembering and those you want to never plant again. By always observing your garden, you will save yourself from having to replace dead and diseased plants or using a ton of water to hydrate an overly thirsty plant. Keeping a record lets you learn from your mistakes and successes, and because gardening is seasonal, it cultivates forgiveness and lets you try again next season if you didn't quite get it right this time.

Stay sharp

Keep your garden tools sharp and clean. Every few weeks I grab a handheld file specifically for sharpening hand pruners and I give my pruners a few drags over the stone. I also clean my pruners with a scouring pad and some warm, soapy water to remove any sap, dirt, or potential pathogens, then wipe the blade dry. In the joints, I apply a lubricant to stop rust and oxidation. On the blade, I lightly apply olive oil. When my clippers get extremely dull, I take them to get professionally sharpened. I also clean off my muddy shovels and trowels at the end of the day

Keeping clippers sharp and clean is an important gardening task that's often overlooked.

with water and dry them with a cotton rag. The benefit of sharp hand pruners is that they make cleaner cuts that heal more efficiently, which creates a healthier plant better able to fight disease, hungry insects, and natural stresses. Plus, sharp pruners prevent blisters and hand strain.

To properly store tools for a long stint, fill a container with vegetable oil mixed with clean construction sand, and dip your clean tools in there. The sand scrubs the metal and the oil stops rust from forming.

If you'll be doing substantial amounts of pruning, invest in a quality holster to house your clippers. While it may cost money up front, you will save money by not having to buy new pruners every time you lose them deep in a shrub somewhere.

winter

If you're like me, you don't just garden in the warm and pretty months. Even if my job didn't require me to garden all year, I definitely would. I honestly enjoy a continuous relationship with plants (though I'll admit to being spoiled living in mild Northern California where I don't have to battle snow or debilitating heat). While winter may be filled with dreary, cold days, there is still something cozy about bundling up and walking the garden, looking for fallen branches and leaves to rake or plants needing a little extra care. If you keep up with maintenance tasks little by little, you can spend more enjoyable time in the yard in the warm months.

SOW TIME In warmer climates, you can get a head start on your planting by sowing cool-weather seeds outdoors. Examples include sweet peas, snapdragons, alyssum, calendula, columbine, and poppies. Many zones

Birds appreciate suet, especially in winter.

can start in February, but seed packets will have specific guidance. In cooler climates, you can start seeds indoors.

OUT OF THE GUTTER Remember to remove leaves from gutters and clean off pathways—wet leaves can be dangerously slippery.

IN THE ORCHARD Avoid pruning plants if frost or snow is expected, but think about pruning fruit trees around February. If frost is forecasted, protect your tender plant children at night with whatever you have on hand—a proper frost cloth or an old bedsheet work just as well.

FEED WITH SEED Don't forget about your feathered friends. Make sure to put out seed and high-fat, energy-packed food like suet for birds who sometimes struggle with foraging in winter. To protect birds from outbreaks of salmonella and other avian diseases, disinfect feeders at least every two weeks. To do this, soak feeders for ten minutes in a 10 percent bleach solution, then scrub, rinse, and dry completely before refilling with fresh seed. Birdbaths should be emptied and cleaned daily. Always wear protective gloves while handling bleach and wash your hands with soap and water after cleaning any feeders or baths.

spring

Spring rivals fall in terms of being a busy garden season. Once the weather and the soil start warming up, both you and the creatures above and below ground get gardening again.

WEED WATCH Water + warmth = weeds. You must jump on weedy invaders before they go to seed and while the ground still has moisture in it to make the weed removal process easier. This means adding mulch to your garden before the weeds infiltrate. If it's too late and you already have a war on your hands, try smothering weeds under layers of newspaper then covering with mulch, compost, or wood chips. For natural weed control, spray undiluted household white vinegar directly and liberally on weeds. You can add a teaspoon of liquid soap or natural dishwashing liquid to help the vinegar spray stick to the foliage. The vinegar will kill the leaves of the plant, but not always the roots, so you may need to reapply. Don't spray vinegar on any plant you don't want damaged. Spray on a hot, sunny day for best results. The acid will scorch the weeds and kill them in a few days.

Spring is when a garden wakes up.

You can also pour boiling water over weeds and cover the scalded area with an old blanket to hold in the heat and finish them off. If all else fails, hungry goats can be rented through special services to mow down large areas of unwanted grass and noxious weeds. This cute method is cost-effective, eco-friendly, and totally entertaining.

LEAK DETECTOR Before turning your irrigation system back on, check the lines for leaks and breaks and open them to clear any settled debris.

FEEDING TIME Feed the soil with copious amounts of organic amendments like compost, blood meal, and bone meal gently mixed together. By amending your soil now, you're giving plants time to access the nutrients before they begin growing in earnest. Organic amendments release nutrients into the soil slower than synthetic ones, which reduces the stress on plants.

THE GREAT DIVIDE If you live in colder climates (zones 3–5) and waited to divide crowded plants, now is the time.

VEGGIE TIME Get your spring vegetable garden going. I find that lettuce planted now will burst before the heat of summer knocks it back. Be aware that while the temperature may be warming above ground, the soil may still be too cold, which will cause plants to struggle. Make sure nighttime temperatures stay consistently at or above 50 degrees F. If you are too eager, start your seeds inside.

FEELING ROSY In zones 1–6, prune roses and feed them with some alfalfa for bloom production and some sprinkles of coffee grounds for nitrogen.

BLOOMS AHEAD Plant summer-blooming bulbs like dahlias, gladiola, and begonias.

TOP COOL-SEASON VEGETABLES

Brassicas (broccoli, cauliflower, and Brussels sprouts, planted as starts)	Peas
	Radish
	Spinach
Lettuce	Swiss chard

STAKE EARLY Some perennials and edibles that grow taller than two feet will benefit from being staked, as their stems aren't equipped to handle high winds and heavy rains and they can get floppy. Unfortunately once stems bend, break, or get all intertwined, it's tricky and frustrating to prop them up again without elaborate and unsightly traction-like set-ups. So plan ahead and get a support system in place. This allows the plants to grow into the support and is easier than trying to jerry-rig a system after the fact, which risks damaging branches and flowers. Also some vegetables and fruits produce a bigger harvest when supported. I use tomato cages for more than propping up tomatoes—try them for supporting raspberries, pole beans, and peas.

Top: Simple bamboo stakes are inexpensive and effective supports.

Above: Stake sedums to support upright growth.

TOP FLOWERING PLANTS TO STAKE EARLY

Blackberry	Peony
Dahlia	Pole bean
Delphinium	Raspberry
Larkspur	Sweet pea
Lily	Tomato
Pea	Zinnia

PRO TIP

Before pruning shrubs in spring, always check for hidden bird nests. If you discover a nest, don't touch it or remove it, and don't worry—most nesting action takes approximately a month from egg laying to fledging, so the wait time isn't long. In the meantime, monitor the progress by reporting your observations to NestWatch.org, which helps scientists track the reproductive success of wild bird populations. It's actually illegal (a violation of the federal Migratory Bird Treaty Act managed by the Fish and Wildlife Service) to disturb any bird nests native to North America. If in question, leave the nest alone.

summer

A summer border
bursting with blooms

If you've prepped your garden beds with compost and mulch and done
the major work in spring, then summer should be mostly about deadheading flowers to promote blooming, perhaps adding more edibles,
and harvesting your bounty.

A summer border
bursting with blooms

ENLIST HELP FROM KIDS
When school let's out, involve kids with the garden chores. This can save you time, help them connect with nature, and teach them valuable gardening skills.

THE EARLY WORM
At the start of summer, plant warm-season vegetables that can handle hot weather and mature quickly, as well as some full-season crops that take ninety days or more to mature.

Kids make captivating garden companions and helpers.

PRUNING PRIORITY Pruning your plants has immediate visual and practical effects in your garden. Not only does deadheading flowers keep plants looking tidy but it also keeps them blooming longer (if you want them to go to seed for next year, stop deadheading certain annuals toward the end of summer). Prune away any weak, spindly, dead, or diseased stems on trees and shrubs. Pruning makes plants more vigorous by concentrating the growth into the wanted stems, and a well-pruned plant uses water more efficiently than a rangy plant, because the roots don't have to feed excess branches and leaves.

To encourage tea roses to see multiple bloom cycles, deadhead spent blossoms before they form rose hips and deadhead at the fifth leaf pointing outward as it's this leaf that has the best bud on it. Cutting roses this way keeps them open at the center for better air circulation.

POT TLC Check on potted plants and make sure they are getting enough water, as they can dry out quickly in summer's heat. Also, feed your pots with compost tea or fish emulsion.

TOP IDEAS TO GET KIDS HELPING IN THE GARDEN

- Pinch faded flowers
- Water potted plants
- Harvest flowers and edibles
- Rake leaves
- Turn the compost heap
- Weed paths and beds
- Thin seedlings
- Hand pick beetles
- Hunt for slugs and snails
- Refill birdbaths, bird feeders, and hummingbird feeders

TOP SUMMER EDIBLES

Bush bean

Carrot

Cucumber

Eggplant

Garlic

Leek

Parsnip

Pepper

Potato

Tomato

fall

Cooler weather ushers in warming autumnal colors.

As the weather cools and harvests turn from sweet fruits to crunchy greens, flowers fade to seedheads, and leaves turn a kaleidoscope of colors, our energy shifts to a more peaceful, cozy rhythm. The garden may be slowing down, but the chores are still numerous, and the work you tackle now will make a huge difference for your spring and summer garden.

Fall is perfect for evaluating your garden, since perennials and shrubs tolerate being moved now and have a longer timeline to re-establish their roots before the stresses of summer set in again.

TOUGH TIMES Prepare and toughen up your plant children for the harshness of winter by not interfering with nature, not deadheading certain flowers like sunflowers and echinacea, and letting seeds naturally form. By resisting the urge to cut back spent stalks, you'll also be providing birds with food through winter when their meal choices and supplies are sparse.

SLOW ON THE H$_2$O Reduce your watering schedule. Cooler fall nights mean less evaporation, which reduces your plants' need for water. You also want your plants to go into dormancy prior to any hard freezes to increase their survival rate.

PLAN PLANTINGS Fall is a great planting time because the soil is still warm enough to encourage root growth and seed germination. Plant trees, perennials, and shrubs in fall so they have the luxury of taking their sweet time to grow slow and strong over winter. This is an especially good time to plant natives. If your goal is to eventually have a drought-tolerant garden, it's best to plan ahead and plant in fall because as the rain sets in, native plant roots get a jumpstart at acclimating to hard, unforgiving local soil.

Let sunflowers go to seed, creating ready-made free feeders for birds to snack on.

Feeling cool

Plant cool-season vegetables that mature in a short or medium length of time. These fall plant friends can withstand frosty weather and, in some cases, hang tight through cold weather. Plus they take up less space than ground-hogging squash and pumpkins.

SLEEPY TIME If you want to put your vegetable beds to sleep instead of planting a fall garden, plant a cover crop (discussed on page 200) to naturally add nutrients to your soil and keep your garden productive.

GO ON THE OFFENSIVE As weather grows more damp, watch for destructive snails and slugs. To catch the night eaters in the act, place lettuce leaves around the garden in the evening and in the wee hours of the morning go on a search-and-destroy mission.

Kale is a super healthy and classic cold-weather crop.

TOP FALL VEGETABLES

Beet	Lettuce
Collard	Onion and shallot
Fennel	Radish
Garlic	Spinach
Kale	

DIVIDE AND CONQUER In warmer climates, fall is the perfect time to divide many spring bloomers and transplant perennials.

CALL IN THE DOCTOR Look for diseased plants afflicted with mildew, black spot, or orange rust. Cut these plants back to give them more sunlight and better air circulation. Remove any affected leaves and any that have fallen on the ground, as they can fester over winter and re-infect the plant. Remember: never add any diseased plants to your compost pile. If you prune diseased plant parts, always disinfect between cuts by wiping your cutting tool with hydrogen peroxide to stop the spread of pathogens.

If perennials, like these lamb's ears, barely grow in a season, it may be a sign it's time to divide.

LEAVE THE LEAVES Fall is synonymous with leaves but please avoid bagging them up and sending them to our crowded landfills. Instead, add them to your compost pile or mow over them and leave them on your lawn as a great nitrogen source.

BYE BYE, BULBS In colder climates, unearth vulnerable summer bulbs like dahlias and store them away in a bucket or box filled with wood shavings. A good place to keep them over winter is in the garage.

HELLO, BULBS Fall is the time to practice delayed gratification and think about what cheery flowers you'd like to see popping up in spring. Shop your local nursery for hardy bulbs to plant in mid to late fall before the ground freezes. Read the label to know how deep to plant your bulbs and plant them with the pointy ends facing up. If you're unsure which end is up, plant them on their side.

TOP BULBS TO PLANT IN FALL

Crocus (*Crocus* spp.)

Daffodil
(*Narcissus* spp.)

Grape hyacinth
(*Muscari* spp.)

Ornamental
flowering onion
(*Allium* spp.)

Siberian squill
(*Scilla* spp.)

Tulip (*Tulipa* spp.)

RELIABLE FALL FLOWERS

Calendula
(*Calendula officinalis*)

Coral bells
(*Heuchera* spp.)

Icelandic poppy
(*Papaver nudicaule*)

Mums
(*Chrysanthemum* spp.)

Pansy
(*Viola ×wittrockiana*)

Pink (*Dianthus* spp.)

Violet (*Viola* spp.)

FLOWER POWER With the display of the summer garden winding down, squeeze one more round of colorful pretties in before the weather turns totally chilly. For the most impact, tuck some festive fall-hued annuals and perennials into pots and garden bed edges.

FEELING HIP Instead of deadheading those decorative rose hips on your rugosa roses and adding them to your compost pile, turn them into vitamin-packed, slightly sweet rose hip tea. Remember to only use rose hips that you are certain have not been sprayed with harmful chemicals. The best time to harvest your rose hips is just after a light frost. Also be sure to use the rose hips right after you pick them to retain their healthy vitamin C content.

In addition to being ornamental, rose hips make a nutritious tea.

Homemade Rose Hip Tea Recipe

INGREDIENTS:
2 teaspoons organic rose hips
1 cup of filtered water

1. Give your rose hips a good rinse with water to remove any dirt or dust.
2. Boil water in a small stainless steel pot (aluminum and copper destroy the vitamin C).
3. Add the rose hips to the water and let them simmer for ten to fifteen minutes.
4. Turn off the heat, let rest for five minutes, then carefully strain the tea into a glass container.
5. Add a variety of natural sweeteners like honey or stevia. I always add a slice of lemon too.

resources

reference books and further reading

SPENDING A GOOD PORTION OF 2020'S INSOLATING QUARANTINE days researching and writing this book wasn't so bad. I perused garden book after garden book while a silly black Labrador named Rubus (yes, the scientific name for blackberry) snuggled at my feet, healing warm nettle tea rested in my cup, and my creative son urged me to leave my work and play basketball. The books listed below guided me as I simplified, condensed, and pruned down my years of gathered info, facts, tips, and know-how and hopefully turned it all into something simple, understandable, and inspiring. Last pro tip? The best place to start a collection of garden literature is to focus on any books, magazines, or online references that speak to your specific region and taste and go from there.

Bay Area Gardening: 64 Practical Essays by Master Gardeners. Traveler's Tales/Solas House. 2005.

The Big Book of Gardening Skills. Garden Way Publishing. 1993.

Benjamin, Joan. *Great Garden Shortcuts: Hundreds of All-New Tips and Techniques That Guarantee You'll Save Time, Save Money, Save Work.* Rodale Press. 1996.

Conran, Terence, *The Essential Garden Book.* Conran Octopus. 1998.

Darke, Rick, and Doug Tallamy. *The Living Landscape: Designing for Beauty and Biodiversity in the Home Landscape.* Timber Press. 2014.

Gershuny, Grace. *Start with the Soil.* Rodale Press. 1993.

Gilbertie, Sal and Sheehan, Larry. *Small-Plot, High-Yield Gardening.* Ten Speed Press. 2010.

Highland, Mark. *Practical Organic Gardening: The No-Nonsense Guide to Growing Naturally.* Cool Springs Press. 2017.

Mizejewski, David. *National Wildlife Federation ®: Attracting Birds,*

Butterflies and other Backyard Wildlife. Expanded Second Edition, Revised. Timber Press. 2019.

The Organic Gardener's Handbook of Natural Pest and Disease Control: A Complete Guide to Maintaining a Healthy Garden and Yard the Earth-Friendly Way. Edited by Fern Marshall Bradley, Barbara W. Ellis and Deborah L. Martin. Rodale Books. 2009.

Peirce, Pamela. *Golden Gate Gardening: The Complete Guide to Year-Round Food Gardening in the San Francisco Bay Area and Coastal California*. Sasquatch Books. 2010.

Pleasant, Barbara, and Martin, L. Deborah. *The Complete Compost Gardening Guide*. Storey Publishing, LLC. 2008

Waldin, Monty. *Biodynamic Gardening: Grow Healthy Plants and Amazing Produce with the Help of the Moon and Nature's Cycles*. DK. 2015.

online learning, shopping & community

Ahsgardening.org

Audubon.org

Foodgatherers.org

Garden.org

Gardeners.com

Groworganic.com

Harmonyfarm.com

Issg.org

Motherearthnews.com

Nwf.org

Passthepistil.com

Planetnatural.com

Rareseeds.com

Reneesgarden.com

acknowledgments

HUMONGOUS HUGS AND KISSES to my boys, Matt and Jack, who granted me the time and space to hunker down and write this book. They were my witty and energetic cheerleaders the entire way. Every day they are my source of humor and humility, and are my honest heroes.

To my mom, the eternal flower, who teaches me so much with her clever, caring, and creative ways.

To my dad, who showed me that it's totally okay, and actually better, to do things differently.

To my sister, Tavia, who thankfully shares a love of plants and will garden with me any time.

A bouquet of thanks to my cooperative clients and neighbors Julie and Jordan, Cathy and Charlie, Jill, Alice and Rick, Megan and Jon, Lisa J., Adam and Marta, and Allison who let their gardens be photographed.

To Kathy Z., who taught me the importance of planting African blue basil and Icelandic poppies.

To Kevin and Xander at Green Jeans Garden Supply, who graciously let me and Emily take photos, and who have always offered the most spectacular plants.

Special credit to my fellow plant enthusiast and friend Emily Murphy, who snapped some of these stellar photographs and kindly shepherded me through this book's creation.

And last, but not least, to the wonderfully supportive team at Timber Press for making this book happen when gardeners perhaps need it the most.

photo credits

Deborah Jones, 6, 7

Emily Murphy, 14, 15, 18 top, 18 middle right, 18 bottom, 21, 22 bottom, 38, 39 right, 40 bottom, 42 top, 44, 46, 48, 50, 55 top, 55 right, 56, 57 top, 57 middle, 57 bottom left, 59 top left, 63 top left, 63 bottom, 66 top, 80 top, 84 right, 97 top, 101, 105, 106, 108, 112, 113, 114, 115 bottom, 117 bottom, 118, 120 bottom, 127, 135, 148, 157 top, 159 bottom, 161, 162, 169, 170, 171, 175, 176, 180, 202, 203, 204, 205, 206, 207, 208, 209, 210, 213, 215, 217, 219, 225, 226, 229 bottom, 232, 237

Kier Holmes, 18 middle left, 20 bottom, 24, 27, 39 left, 40 top, 41 left, 42 bottom, 45 top, 52, 54, 55 bottom left, 57 bottom right, 59 top middle, 60 top, 65, 66 bottom, 71 left, 72 right, 80 middle and bottom, 92, 95, 98, 99 top, 100, 115 top, 117 top, 120 top, 121, 122, 125, 133, 134, 136 right, 138, 139, 147, 149, 157 bottom, 158, 159 top, 163 top right, 168, 172, 173, 184, 185, 189, 190, 191, 201, 222, 229 top, 230, 235, 236, 239

Wirestock, Dreamstime, 59 bottom right

Alamy
A Garden, 43 right
Adrian Sherratt, 99 bottom
Andreas von Einsiedel, 23, 77 bottom
BIOSPHOTO, 110–111, 116, 234

Botany vision, 131, 163 top left
ClassicStock, 137
Deborah Vernon, 89 right, 89 bottom left
imageBroker, 59 bottom left
Jacek Wac, 31
Mark Bolton Photography, 88
Panther Media GmbH, 41 right
Paul Maguire, 119
Photimageon, 89 top left
RM Floral, 59 top right
Steve Hawkins Photography, 90
Trevor Chriss, 227
wordplanet, 136 left
YAY Media AS, 124

GAP
Andrea Jones, 86 right
Andrew Maybury, 10–11, 63 top right
Brent Wilson, 28, 73
Brian North, 83 right
Carole Drake, 74
Chris Harris, 70
Clive Nichols, 68–69
Elke Borkowski, 19, 83 bottom left, 153 bottom middle, 192
Fiona McLeod, 153 middle middle
Friedrich Strauss, 22 top
GAP Photos, 17, 81, 84 left, 87 left, 144, 146, 153 bottom right
Graham Strong, 78, 153 middle right, 164, 238
Hanneke Reijbroek, 43 left
Howard Rice, 153 bottom left, 156 bottom
J S Sira, 16, 60 bottom
Janet Loughrey, 75 bottom
Jerry Harpur, 12, 47
Jerry Pavia, 153 top middle

Jo Whitworth, 153 top right
Jonathan Buckley, 153 top left
Juliette Wade, 145
Karen Chapman, 72 left, 76
Leigh Clapp, 156 top
Manuela Goehner, 75 top
Mark Bolton, 152
Nicola Stocken, 4–5, 29, 64, 83 top left, 86 left, 87 right, 132, 182 left
Pernilla Hed, 153 middle left, 199
Richard Bloom, 2, 36, 102, 142
Visions, 59 middle right

iStock
beekeepx, 94
bgwalker, 53
fotolinchen, 166 bottom, 231
Lludmyla Lludmyla, 62
lublub, 107
LukeLuke68, 163 bottom left
Marion Carniel, 35
middelveld, 91 bottom left
Mkovalevskaya, 25, 92
Olga Chetvergova, 91 top
OlgaKorica, 179
Orchidpoet, 45
Rafmaster, 85 bottom
shippee, 186–187
squirrel77, 58
Тодорчук Екатерина, 20 middle right
Ulrike Leone, 32
wayra, 154

Shutterstock
Andris Tkacenko, 126
Bachkova Natalia, 150
Beach Creatives, 109
COULANGES, 59 middle left
Danny Ye, 183

Fenneke Smouter, 51

Gonzalo de Miceu, 91 bottom right

Helga_foto, 233

HollyHarry, 85 top

Kuttelvaserova Stuchelova, 20 top

leopictures, 32

Martina Unbehauen, 97 bottom

PhillipsC, 128 top

photowind, 163 bottom right

Pitsanu Kraichana, 71 right

Rose Makin, 77 top

Sarycheva Olesia, 177

Shannon Mendez, 20 left

sirtravelalot, 26

Stanislav71, 182 right

Supaleka_P, 166 top

svf74, 59 middle

topimages, 59 bottom middle

Zhiltsov Alexandr, 128 bottom

index

KIER HOLMES is a garden designer and writer with bylines in *Martha Stewart*, *Better Homes and Gardens*, *Gardenista*, *Sonoma Magazine*, *Marin Magazine*, and *Sunset Magazine*, among other publications. She is also a children's garden and science educator and gives regular talks on various gardening topics to adults at the Mill Valley Public Library. She grew up in Marin County and has designed and maintained gardens there for over twenty years, focusing on chemical-free, richly textured, and visually dynamic spaces.